Entertaining and very informative to a "small farm kid" of southern Ohio and Indiana origin. The contrasts are remarkable, the similarities startling.

---Ruth Davison, retired librarian

* * *

Congratulations! This book is so interesting and told in a friendly manner just like you. You have captured beautifully so much of you—a record book that will be preserved in history and appreciated by unnumbered readers.

---Pauline W. Caldwell, R.N., B.S.N., M.L.S.

* * *

Elsieferne Stout has written an engaging book that tells her story of growing up and at the same time gives us of glimpses of an almost forgotten way of life. The way her family lived when she was a child had more in common with the pioneers than with our lives today.

---Al Hein

* * *

Elsieferne Stout shares with us the minute details of the equipment and processes of living and farming in the early Nebraska settlement.

---Martha Dawson

* * *

This book gives a very personal view of the author's early life on a farm on the Nebraska plains.

---Jim Dawson

* * *

This book is on amazing recall of homesteading in Nebraska, the machinery, the tools and the stalwart people who used them.

---Wynona Springer

GITTY UP! ——

——WHOA!

Elsieferne V. Stout

authorHOUSE®

AuthorHouse™
1663 Liberty Drive, Suite 200
Bloomington, IN 47403
www.authorhouse.com
Phone: 1-800-839-8640

First published by AuthorHouse 9/5/2007

ISBN: 978-1-4343-1809-1 (sc)

Library of Congress Control Number: 2007904248

Printed in the United States of America
Bloomington, Indiana

This book is printed on acid-free paper.

This book is dedicated to the brave determined individuals, the settlers,
who left their families and homes of comfort and
convenience in their search for the dream.
These dreams of a home in a new area created excitement,
adventure and new horizons.
They traveled in horse-drawn wagons many miles under difficult conditions.
How disappointing when they learned that "The Great Plains"
was a semi-arid area,
and not a gardener's paradise.
The many hardships endured, as the travelers slowly moved
into the new lands, were inconceivable. Those who persevered
attained their dreams and settled the great prairies.
Horses provided the means for the settlers to relocate to land westward
beyond the Mississippi River. And were the sustainable power needed to
maintain agriculture in the grasslands.

BOOKS

My Pioneer Ancestors

Dundy County Babe

THE COVER

GITTY UP—(spelled phonically) as was spoken by Author's parents along with a quick slap of the reins on the horses' backs signaled for the team to move forward.

WHOA!—was the stop command along with a tightening of the reins which exerted pressure on the bits in the horses' mouths, and they stopped.

The Photo   The farm as it appeared when the Author's parents purchased it in 1911. The house was the birth place and home of the Author for 21 years. Just to the right of the house was the tool shed mentioned in the story. The well, horses and buggies, a wagon and the horse barn complete the pioneer barnyard. The Author's father and mother (to the left) are in the photo. The other man's identity is unknown.

ACKNOWLEDGEMENTS

Many thanks to Al Hein, Jim and Martha Dawson, Wynona Springer, Jean Sebeok, Mark Day, Pauline Caldwell, Ruth Davison, Art Haldeman, and other friends for their help.

CONTENTS

INTRODUCTION XIII

CHAPTER I   MY HOME AND MY FAMILY 1

CHAPTER II   FARM BUILDINGS AND ANIMAL HOMES 27

CHAPTER III   NON-FARMING ACTIVITIES ON THE FARM 41
    Butchering 42
    Cattle 46
    Fences 49

CHAPTER IV   FARMING 53
    Planting 54
    Cultivating 56
    Harvesting 57
    Haying 61

CHAPTER V   OTHER ACTIVITIES 65
    Hunting 65
    Food Preservation 66
    Soap making 67
    Voting 68

CHAPTER VI   WILDLIFE 69

CHAPTER VII   PIONEER MEDICINE 75

CHAPTER VIII   FASHIONS 79

CHAPTER IX   RECREATION 85

CHAPTER X   SCHOOL 91

EPILOGUE 97

ABOUT THE AUTHOR 101

ILLUSTRATIONS

Author with six horse team..xv

Well making tools xvii

Homestead 1908...xxii

Author, vines and gas pump 2

Hoosier Cabinet... 11

My brothers and their car.. 17

My farm home 22

Family photo... 25

Sketch of sprayer 28

Brother Alvin with colt... 30

Illustration of pump jack... 47

Sketches of gates... 51

Photo of hand corn sheller 54

Photos of husking tools 58

Photo of Author age 4 79

Author's brothers 1917... 80

INTRODUCTION

As immigrants arrived in the United States from England and Europe, they first settled along the east coast. Gradually, the settlers crept westward, but few had ventured west of the Mississippi River. The west coastal areas of this large country contained few settlements until the California Gold Rush of 1849. News of rich farmland in Washington and Oregon attracted many. However, the vast prairie in the central part of the country remained grassland, occupied for the most part by the many Indian tribes, the Native Americans.

To encourage settlements in the prairie, Congress passed the Homestead Act in 1862. This law offered ownership of a quarter section of land to anyone, who filed a claim, improved the land, and lived on it for five years. Improvements included a well, a home, and farming of at least five acres. (Land was identified by sections, which was divided into four equal parts. A quarter of a section was 160 acres.) In addition, the settler was required to understand English, and be a United States citizen. If the settler were not a citizen, he or she was required to become a citizenship before a "patent" or deed was issued by the United States Government. The land was free except for a small filing fee.

This offer attracted people everywhere, and especially by the information, "the land is so rich that one needs only stick a plant into the soil and it will grow abundantly." However, this information was flawed, especially for the semi-arid Great Plains region, which had little rainfall. Soon many settlers were disillusioned with homesteading. After many months of hard labor, and the heartache of crop failures, many settlers packed their possessions and sadly moved away.

The soil across Nebraska varied. The north central part of the state contained the largest sand hill area of the United States, aptly known today as "The Sand Hills." In addition, the soil in Dundy County, which is located in the south-southwest corner of the state, the county of my birth, contained a small pocket of that sandy soil. The sandy soil areas of Nebraska were more suited to grazing instead of farming. Yet, a few miles from my parents' farm, the soil was called "hard ground." This soil, when wet became a slippery muck, in contrast to wet sand that packed down for firm footing. Wheeled vehicles were more difficult to maneuver in dry sandy soil.

These brave settlers traveled westward in covered wagons or "prairie schooners" pulled by horses. A "prairie schooner" was a shallow wagon with attached arches covered with white cloth for protection from the weather for people and their possessions. Once a claim was filed, a house and a well soon appeared.

The weather was smothering hot in summer and equally bitter cold in winter with a generous supply of strong wind the year around. The lack of rivers or creeks meant there was also a lack of trees for building homes. Since trees or stones were not available to build a house, the homesteaders used the only material available—sod. Short curly buffalo grass (great for grazing) grew in this area. The grass roots were densely entwined in the soil; this made the soil difficult to penetrate with a steel plow. However, this soil when cut into brick-shaped pieces, became an inexpensive material used to build houses and barns.

These "bricks," laid grass side down, formed the walls. Wood, when available, lined openings for the windows and a door. These settlers used what ever was available for the rafters and foundation for the roof. The "shingles" were bricks of sod laid with the grass side up. The white canvas from the wagons became the coverings for the windows and door.

Soddies, though not very clean or sanitary by today's standards, were inexpensive to build, and well insulated—cool in summer and warm in winter. They were tornado-proof. The disadvantages of these earthen homes were the need for frequent repairs especially after hard rains, and the invasions of insects, rodents, and snakes. After wood became more available as a building material, "soddies" became a house of the past.

The home of my birth and my home for twenty-one years was a simple three-room frame farmhouse with an enclosed back porch. The enclosed back porch or fourth room had a cement floor and contained the running water system, washing machine and cream separator. However, this room was never heated. This house, though simple, was a grand house or a mansion when compared to a soddie.

HORSES

Horses and mules provided the power to pull the wagons or "prairie schooners" across the prairies for these westward bound travelers. They were man's best traveling companion. When treated kindly, these animals responded with great strength doing their best for their "masters." However, sometimes these "masters" expected the horses to perform impossible feats.

When the horses refused to cross into dangerous terrain pulling the heavy wagons or refused to enter unsafe turbulent waters, their masters tried to force the animals forward with severe lashes with a horsewhip. The results were drowning, and injuries to both the humans and the horses.

After the homesteaders had reached their destinations, gratitude for their horses was shown by the settlers with "dug outs" or "soddies" built first for the horses. This not only protected the horses (man's special companions) from the severe weather but from the wild animals and Indians.

Horses continued to be important for the settlers. They pulled the steel plows that skimmed the sod from the land for the homes, pulled the machines for planting and harvesting, the wagons to get supplies, and transportation. Horses, also, provided a pleasure ride. Horses enabled the settlers to survive.

A team of six horses stand at attention focusing on the Author (age 14) wearing blue and white stripped overalls.

THE WELL

One of the requirements of the Homestead Act, after the selected claim was registered, was to dig a well. This was essential, as many of the homesteads in Dundy County were miles from the closest stream. Filling barrels with water and hauling it a great distance was not practical.

The sandy soil in Dundy County, Nebraska required few well digging tools. These tools included—a sand bucket, pipe dogs, three 20 foot long two by fours (2x4's were wood cut to the size of two inches thick and four inches wide), a hoist (a lifting device), and pipe wrenches.

The sand bucket was a heavy iron cylinder, four inches in diameter, and about five feet long with a sharp bottom edge that cut into the soil. Flanges inside the bucket held the soil. The pipe dogs, two small iron jaws attached to a 2x12 x 24 inch piece of wood held the pipe. These iron jaws temporarily held the pipe as the pieces were attached together with a coupling. The cylinder, which fit inside the pipe, was attached to the rod. This rod along with the pipe was attached to the iron hand pump. The two large heavy pipe wrenches (with 24-inch handles) were used to connect the pipes together.

Materials needed for the well included several 20-foot sections (pieces) of galvanized iron pipe with couplings, the cylinder (which contained the valve that held the water), sections of casing, and the rod.

To dig a well, the sand bucket, attached to a rope, was dropped from the derrick. This derrick was made with three 2x4x20 foot long timbers bolted together at one end with the three free ends spread apart at the bottom to form a tripod base. This tripod was set over the chosen spot for the well. The sand bucket dropped from the top of the tripod into the hole. Soil caught in inside flanges was removed from the hole. As the hole grew deeper, the casing was pushed into the ground to hold the soil in place. When the casing hit gravel, a good supply of water was expected. Then the pipe was lowered into the casing. It was held temporarily with the pipe dogs until it was extended with more pipe and couplings to reach into the water at the bottom of the casing. The pipe was secured to the hand pump. The cylinder with the rod attached was lowered inside the pipe. Then the rod was attached to the hand pump, or to the windmill gearbox shaft.

Presto! Now it was possible to pull cool water from deep in the earth. A person could lift the long handle of a hand pump (that action pushed open the valve in the cylinder at the bottom of the well), and as the handle went down, water was pulled into the pipe. Repeating this process rapidly resulted in the water rising in the pipe and was soon flowing from the pump spout. Our 50 foot well provided plenty of "sand hill" water. "Sand hill" water was soft, low in minerals, and tasted wonderful. The Dundy County settlers bragged about their great tasting "sand hill" water. They believed no other water could match that flavor.

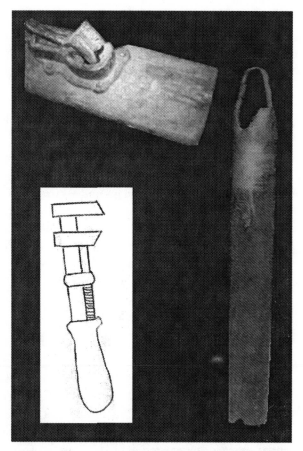

Well making tools.(l-r) Monkey wrench (antique pipe wrench), pipe dogs (upper left) and sand bucket

I never actually observed a well as it was dug originally but I heard the conversations between my brothers and my dad. I watched them "clean the well" near the house. The process was similar to the well digging process. They pulled the pipe up to get to the cylinder, and then remove the leathers from inside the cylinder and replaced them with new ones. The leather gaskets, called "leathers," made a tight seal inside the cylinder to retain the quantity of water as it was drawn in with each lowering of the pump handle until the pipe was filled to overflowing. They never wanted me near when they worked on the well. Guess they were afraid I would be in the wrong place at the wrong time and I probably would have been. I watched safely from the back door of the house.

The well needed cleaning when the water was no longer clear but was filled with sand. The sand was drawn into the well at the bottom of the casing.

When very little water was brought up, new leather gaskets were needed. Replacing the leather gaskets or cleaning the well was a dreaded task that had to be done regardless of the weather. Sometimes a well filled with sand, or ran dry, and then a new well was necessary.

"Water Witches" frequently were consulted to find a good location for a well. These "witches" claimed they could locate underground water using a small "Y" shaped twig. I heard reports that the twigs from willow trees were preferred because—willows grow best near water. These "witches" held the "Y" with one small branch loosely in each hand and the larger branch horizontal as they slowly walked over the ground. When the larger branch turned downward of its own accord, they claimed that was the location of underground water. Did it work? Does that sound too good to be true? It has never been proven to be foolproof. I never observed a "Water Witch" at work but I heard people described the process many times. I wished I could have observed one.

FARMING CHALLENGES

The weather controls crop production. During the homesteading days, agriculture was a high-risk occupation. The crops meant survival for the livestock and the pioneer and his family. With little capital to buy seed, feed for the livestock, and needs for the family in times of crop failures, a good crop was essential. A good harvest required favorable weather for planting, growing and harvesting. A good harvest meant survival.

Spring planting—adequate precipitation was necessary for corn seed to sprout and grow. Control of the spring insects—cut worms cut the tender plants just under the soil. Warm temperatures were necessary. Sometimes a blast of cold Canadian air swooped down and froze the tender plants, and then the crop was gone. Later, as the corn grew tall, and was seen above the dirt ridges formed by the lister, the farmer believed he would have a good crop "If the corn was knee high by the fourth of July." However, before a humid day retired, the hot temperature could suddenly be "wiped out" as black swirling clouds with hail swollen gale-like winds filled the sky. In a few minutes, the promising harvest was a total loss as the hail pounded the plants into the ground.

Insects often prevailed during the summer growing season. The cutworms ate the tender shoots of the sprouting corn hidden under the soil. Later in the growing season, the corn earworm invaded the forming kernels ruining many rows of corn on the cob as it consumed the kernels. Diseases like smut (kernels of corn affected with smut became black powder) and rust both affected the production. Weeds stole the scant moisture. The lack of adequate rain and wind during pollination affected size of the crop. Hot temperatures for months and months yielded drought.

Many of the pioneers, former residents of European countries, farmed their newly acquired land using familiar methods. This included plowing, disking, or harrowing to break up the chunks of sod before planting. The entwined buffalo grass roots made the soil difficult to prepare for farming. However, after a few years under cultivation, the soil revealed its true nature—it was very sandy.

The weather in Plains States was controlled by the air currents, which flowed over the Rocky Mountains. These air currents sucked up the light dry sandy soil creating dust storms. No one realized that the farming methods that were used elsewhere caused critical problems with the Dundy County sandy soil.

A drought occurred in "The Great Plains" (this included Nebraska) during the 1930's. After months of below normal rainfall, crop failure followed year after year. The natural flow of the hot dry winds picked up the loose dry soil in the Plains States forming clouds of dust that rolled miles and miles across the nearly flat land. The airborne sand and dust was deposited everywhere including inside the houses. It left many things partially buried. The plants could not survive. The results—crop failure. The disillusioned settlers abandoned their homesteads and left for other areas.

Breathing the dust-ladened air caused health problems for the men and women who worked out in the fields. Years later, after health care became available in the Dust Bowl states, X-rays revealed that breathing the dust-laden air had caused dust deposits in the lungs. This dust was the probable cause of their breathing problems.

During the drought years, insects wrecked havoc on the growing crops. Grasshoppers created the worst insect threat that I recall. One year they were so numerous that they even chewed on the fence posts. That year the chickens, who favored grasshopper meals, were so tired of the flying insects that they ignored them.

The Agricultural Adjustment Act, a government program, supplied a poisonous mash (sawdust laced with a strong poison and flavored with banana oil) free to the farmers who scattered it at ends of the rows in the cultivated fields and along fences rows where livestock would not graze. The poison in the mash was strong and so effective that after scattering it barehanded a few times, my right hand swelled up so much I could not close it enough to do my usual milking chores.

Indeed the life of homesteaders was challenging with hard labor from dawn to dusk, isolation and far from family, friends and neighbors. They had to be self-sufficient, and depended on no one. Horses provided the power for farming, and transportation. Few doctors were available; grocery stores as we have today did not exist. There was no electricity. Indeed, they were determined and many survived on their free land—their dream, their homes.

* * *

Railroads came to Nebraska in the late 1800's. The route of Burlington Railroad connected towns and cities in the eastern part of Nebraska from Omaha (on Missouri River) though the state on a line near the Kansas-Nebraska border westward to Denver, Colorado. This meant that lumber, tin and other building supplies were available. Livestock and grain were shipped to the markets in the east. People traveled in comfort riding in the closed passenger cars of the trains pulled by coal burning engines.

* * *

The Republican River flowed from Colorado through the northwest corner of Kansas into Dundy County, Nebraska. The riverbed was about three miles north of the Nebraska-Kansas state line. The town of Benkelman was built near this river. In 1935, the Dundy County residents living near the Republican River suffered a horrendous surprise flood.

The small village of Parks, (about 15 miles west of Benkelman) was located in a low valley near the Republican River. On May 31, the Parks residents were awakened in the middle of the night and encouraged to evacuate their homes immediately. They were told to seek higher ground because a wall of water was speeding towards the sleeping village. Unusual heavy rains had fallen in Colorado upstream from Parks and Benkelman had caused the Republican River water to stretch beyond its banks. The villagers scoffed at this news! A flood! That was impossible in this dry land as that spring had been extremely dry with many dust storms.

Regretfully, many people lost their lives. Their homes were destroyed by the swirling churning flood waters. Hundreds of livestock drown. Houses and other shattered buildings lay everywhere. Pieces of buildings and clothing hung everywhere on the uprooted and standing trees. Crops in and near the river bottom were destroyed.

My parents and I viewed the horrific destruction along the river from the highway that connected Benkelman and Parks. As my dad surveyed the destruction, he almost drove into the huge gapping hole where the highway had been. Even after seeing the appalling destruction, it was still difficult to believe that a flood was possible in this area.

1908 Homestead

My father's homestead in 1908. Note the hay stacks to the left of the barn. A small shed seen to the left of the barn roof was probably a tool shed. To the center is the two-room house (Dad moved this house to the farm he bought in 1911. It was made into a car shed for the Model T car.) The horse barn was shelter for the horses and mules. The windmill and fences are in the background to the left. In the foreground (l-r) on horseback: Sadie Graham (my mama's best friend), Lydia Grams (my mama) riding side saddle, the young man with the colt is unknown, as is the man just behind him. Ellis Mendenhall (my dad) sits on the mower with a team of mules. A buggy top is behind these mules. The wood to the right edge of the picture was a water trough. Sagebrush and yucca plants dot the grass land.

CHAPTER I

MY HOME

Come! Visit this home of my birth, it is a small simple house built in the early 1900's. The walk from the sandy driveway to the open yard gate passes the grape vine that grows at the base of the windmill. The beautiful clusters of purple concord grapes hide under the large green silver grape leaves of late summer. I relished eating the grapes right from the vine. Yum! Oh, so sweet to taste! I didn't care if the grapes left my lips and tongue discolored and purple. The delectable juice from these grapes made yummy jelly and jam. That jelly was so tempting that once in awhile I slipped into the cellar to eat the jelly from a jar with my finger. Did I confess when Mama wondered why some jars were sticky on the outside when I brought them to the kitchen in preparation for canning the next summer? Why would I? How I loved the grape jelly on Mama's fresh baked bread!

To the left of the open yard gate, a hand-operated gasoline pump stood above the underground storage tank. I recall the gasoline delivery truck delivered gasoline when I was around three years old. Those gasoline delivery trucks always had a chain that dragged on the road. The chain attached to the truck frame in the back always puzzled me. One day, when I was older, I asked my brother, Alvin, "Why do those trucks have chains dragging on the ground?"

"Sis that chain grounds any sparks from the truck to prevent an explosion." he proudly replied. Fact or fiction? I never knew.

**Author, age 9 stands beside the ivy vine near the hand
operated gas pump near the front yard gate**

Mama planted small Chinese elm trees within the fence of the dry sandy yard. She said, "I'll cut both ends out of a gallon can, then bury the tin cylinder half-way in the ground near each tree. The water will seep directly to the roots. Now you fill the cans with water every day." I dreaded that daily task every summer beginning when I was four or five years old.

The windmill, which pumped our water, stood to the right. The big eight-foot metal wheel, with slightly angled galvanized metal fan-shaped blades, caught the wind, which turned the wheel, and activated gears in the gearbox perched atop the tall wooden tower. This action started the process of drawing the water up from deep in the earth. The big galvanized metal tail turned the wheel to keep it facing the wind, so the slightest breeze activated the wheel and pumped the water.

A wooden stick, hinged to one leg of the tower six to seven feet above the ground, was connected to the tail with a long number nine wire. When the stick was pulled down against the tower leg, the tail folded beside the big wheel. This shut the windmill off. A number nine wire loop encircled the tower leg; it was slipped over the wooden stick to keep the tail parallel to the wheel. The windmill was shut off when the wind was blowing extremely hard or when water was overflowing the stock tank. The wind was a free power source.

The wooden box at the base of the windmill concealed the large galvanized metal barrel that contained the water drawn from deep inside the earth. We kept a tin cup inside this box for the convenience of travelers who stopped for a drink of fresh cool water. Gravel surrounded the barrel to prevent the water from freezing during the bitterly cold winters and to keep the water cool during the hot summers. The windmill provided the water supply for the household and livestock.

* * *

The low wooden porch, the approach to the back door of the house, helped to keep the sand and snow out of the house. This porch provided a convenient storage place for large tall tin cans filled with chicken feed.

I stood on this porch early one cool June morning struggling to open a can of feed for a special little chick. It was hungry and begged for its special treats. Suddenly its begging changed to chatterings of fear!

Mama was in the house. She quickly stepped to the back door curious to see the cause for chick's chatterings. She was shocked—just behind my bare feet was a coiled rattlesnake warming itself in the hot sun. Its rattle-tipped tail extended above its coiled body. "Freeze!" she commanded. Surprised. I did not move. Moments later, she came around the house with a garden hoe and killed the eight-rattle rattlesnake. How thankful I was that I never stepped back, and that the chick sounded the warning. That day, I called chick "My guardian angel."

* * *

Step carefully through the back door into the "water room." In this room was our "unique running water system." My dad slanted the cement floor from the base of the cream separator and the wooden water barrel so all the liquid that spilled on the floor would drain to the dip directly in front of the door with no outlet drain. Wet feet would be the result if any liquid pooled in the dip. I never learned why my dad designed the floor this way. Nobody liked to step into a puddle of water and no one liked to mop up the pool of water.

The water room's green calcimined walls gave the room a cool fresh clean smell. Calcimine was an inexpensive lime-type whitewash for plastered walls, but it was not washable. It was available in white or pastel colors. Mama chose the green calcimine to use on the "water room" and the bedroom walls.

A large wooden barrel in the water room held the inside water supply. The water siphoned from the metal barrel outside at the base of the windmill, through an underground pipe into the inside barrel. Then it trickled through a small short length of pipe near the top of the barrel into the 2x12x12 inch wooden trough. The water in the trough kept our cream and milk cool in crockery or stoneware jars. An old plate covered each jar to keep out the dust and dirt. Eggs were stored on the cool floor underneath the trough. That was our only form of refrigeration; it probably compared to a "well house."

The water siphoned, through a short pipe that extended a few inches up from the bottom of the trough underground to the stock tank by the horse barn. It was wonderful to have running water inside the house. This labor saving arrangement liberated us from many trips outside in freezing cold weather to pump water, and then carry it into the house. I have no idea who invented this unique water system, but it was very convenient to have an abundant supply of water inside the house—a luxury few pioneer homes had.

A small pipe inserted at the floor level in the wall in the corner of this room under the water trough allowed overflowing water to drain outside, instead of running over the water room floor. A small garter snake and a mouse obtained entrance into the water room through this pipe. Mama said, "I'll stop that." She put some window screen wire over the pipe, which prevented the invasion of these intruders.

On washday, it was a blessing to have the water inside the house. We only had to carry water from the barrel to the copper wash boiler that we set on the kitchen range. With a hot fire, hot water was soon available for the laundry. The water left in the wooden barrel was always adequate for other household uses. (The wash boiler and the washtubs were stored outside hanging on nails on the north side of the house when not in use.)

I will never forget the only time when my Aunt Susan (Mama's older sister), a Seventh Day Adventist, visited us. It was a Saturday—wash day. She sat in the rocking chair, in the living room corner of the kitchen, watching us as we filled the copper wash boiler that sat on the stove with water from the barrel. She did not offer to help, but we did not expect any help, as she was our guest. Later, she went to get a drink from the water barrel. "Oh," she said, surprised at seeing the barrel full of water, "I would have helped you carry the water in, but you know this is my Sabbath, and I can't work."

"Oh, no," Mama said. "We didn't fill the barrel. It filled automatically because the windmill was running and pumping water." Aunt Susan was puzzled as Mama explained how our running water system worked. Aunt Susan, who lived on a cattle ranch in Montana, was very impressed.

* * *

The cream separator stood in front of the water barrel. The fresh milk was poured through a large strainer. (A small piece of a flour sack fabric was stretched and held taut on the bottom of the strainer with a ring that slipped around the bottom of the strainer. Straining the milk removed any dirt or sticks that had fallen in the milk.) Now the milk was in the large open tank on top of the separator. As the handle of the hand-operated separator was turned, the milk swirled around and around inside the separator, the cream rose to the top and trickled out through the top spout into a crockery jar that set on a shelf. The milk drained from a larger spout into a milk bucket that sat on the floor. The cream, stored in stoneware jars, sat in the cool water trough. The cream when sour replaced butter on the homemade bread. Sometimes we used part of the skimmed milk for cottage cheese. We used a little of the skimmed milk in the cooking but milk was never served with our meals. The surplus milk was fed to the hogs. We milked six or eight cows night and morning.

After we had collected the cream for several days, we poured it into five or ten-gallon metal cream cans. We took these cans of cream to Benkelman, Nebraska and shipped them by rail to the Hastings Creamery, Hastings, Nebraska where it was made into butter. We received a check by mail for the cream. (Uncle Al at the Hastings Creamery sent me a birthday card each New Years' Day until I was twelve years old. Sometimes he sent a little gift. One gift I still have was a wooden cross puzzle.)

* * *

Sharing space in this small room was our square-tub gasoline-powered Maytag washing machine with a power wringer. On washday, we pulled the washer out from the storage space near the water trough. The Briggs and Stratton motor had a long flexible metal exhaust pipe, which was kept tightly coiled for storage. We uncoiled the flexible pipe and placed the unattached end outside through the open doors (the wooden back door and the screen door) to keep the carbon dioxide fumes from the burning gasoline out of the house. We set a bench that held two round galvanized washtubs of fresh cool rinse water next to the washer. The clothes, white clothes were boiled and then were washed first in the hot lye soapsuds and then run through the wringer into the first tub of rinse water. The clothes were rinsed thoroughly. Then they were run through the wringer into the last rinse. Bluing was in the last rinse water to keep the whites—bright white. The clothes were run through the wringer a third time into the clothes basket. Now the clothes were ready to be hung on the outside clothesline. Our colored clothes followed the white clothes in the washing with the overalls and rags in the last wash.

All the laundry hung outside to dry—winter and summer. On sunny breezy days, the clothes dried quickly with a fresh clean smell, and were soft and fluffy (Fabric softeners were unheard of at that time in history.) In winter, the heaviest garments quickly froze solid. We brought these frozen garments into the house and hung them on the prongs attached on the wall behind the kitchen range where they soon dried.

* * *

On the south side of the water room the "Chore clothes," special garments worn only when doing the chores, hung on hooks and nails in the solid clapboard-sided wall. Wearing chore clothes kept the barnyard odors and the cattle lice from our regular clothing.

Small tools were stored on the narrow shelves attached to the wall in the corner behind the outside door. One frequently used tool was the soldering iron and the spool of lead solder with a liquid acid core. When a pin-sized hole appeared in a tin milk bucket, it was soldered closed with a little solder and the hot soldering iron. I do not recall how but Mama heated that iron in the kitchen range firebox. If a larger hole appeared in a galvanized washtub, solder would not always seal the hole. Then a thin washer (a small circle of metal with a small hole in the center) was placed inside the tub and another washer was laid on the outside and a very small bolt was inserted then a nut tightened to pull the washers together for a water tight seal. Patched buckets and tubs saved the cost of new items.

On the floor near this wall, we kept our overshoes and the "shoe last" and "stand" used for repairing shoes. The "stand" was a flat iron base that sat on the floor with an upright bar about two feet tall. The top of the bar stand was notched to anchor the "shoe last." The "shoe last" was a foot-shaped iron form that fit on top of the "stand." A shoe was slipped over the "last" to replace the leather sole, or rubber heels, or add metal clips to the heels. Small shoe nails were used for both the soles and heels. Our leather shoes had leather soles. The soles wore out before the shoe was out-grown or the leather top wore out. Three "lasts" were in the set. The largest "last" was for men, a medium-sized one for women, and a smaller one for children.

Sometimes the upper part of the shoe leather needed patching. Lightweight leather was used. Holes were punched in the leather shoe upper and in the leather for the patch with an awl, a tool with a sharp metal needle-like point anchored in a wooden handle, made it easier to sew. (This awl is part of my sewing equipment.) A needle, specially designed to sew leather, was threaded with waxed thread and was used to hand-stitch the patch onto the leather of the shoe. Both of my parents did the shoe repairs.

When I was old enough, I replaced the rubber heels and metal heel caps on my own shoes. The shoe repair supplies, including the tack hammer, were stored in a hand-made galvanized metal box about 18 inches square, and kept on the small bottom shelf. (I still have the little hammer that was part of the shoe repair supplies.)

Various larger items were stored on the long shelf above the clothes hooks. The brass blowtorch, which burned white gasoline for fuel, occupied space on this shelf. Just below this long shelf, two spike nails held an unloaded 12-gauge shotgun. Another unloaded 12-gauge shotgun and an unloaded 410-gun stood with butt-end down on the cement floor in the corner of this room nearest the kitchen. The red and green shells with brass caps for these guns were on the highest small shelf behind the outside door.

* * *

Step up, one step into a large room with a linoleum covered floor. This was the kitchen, dining, and living room. The big black cast iron Home Comfort range, our cook stove and heat source for this room (only room normally heated) sat near this entrance. In the winter, the aroma of coffee simmering in the blue-gray enameled coffee pot welcomed everyone along with the singing teakettle. A whiff of the heat and the coffee encircled everyone who entered the kitchen from the cold frosty outside.

The top of the stove had six round metal lids with special indentations. A special tool fit into the indentations to lift the lids. Usually only the lid to the left and in front of the stove was lifted to place fuel into the firebox. With a poker, the burning materials were rearranged in the firebox. The smoke-filled hot air circulated to the right, over the oven, and down the right side of the oven to the exit behind the oven. This exit extended into the stovepipe and chimney that was located at the back of the stove.

Soot and light ash fell from the hot air as it followed the exit route. When smoke began curling up and out from under the metal lids, Mama said, "It's time to clean this smoky monster on the inside." She removed the metal lids above the oven area, and used a small rectangular metal scraper attached to a long black rod to scrap the black soot and ash dust towards the right side of the oven. She closed the lids above the oven, and removed the ones nearest the right side of the stove. Again, she scraped the soot and ash collection down into the opening inside the right side of the stove and scraped the both sides of the space on the right side of the stove. Mama opened the little rectangular door below the oven door then scraped out the accumulation of soot and ashes in a flat pan. This pan looked like an old blackened tin pan that had been formerly been used for baking. This process was repeated several times a year.

Step-back, look at this stove from the front; four doors were visible. The largest was the near square shaped metal oven door. Just below the oven door was a small narrow rectangular door used to clean the soot and ashes that accumulated around the oven. To the left of the oven door was a smaller upright rectangular door. This door concealed the ash bin. Just above this ash bin was a square shaft. With a special wrench that fit on this shaft, the grates were turned to allow the ashes to fall into the ashbin. Above this door was a smaller square door, with hinges on the bottom; it concealed a small air draft opening for the firebox. This door was usually open.

I recall seeing small scraps of shucks from the corncobs fall onto this door as the cobs were placed into the firebox. I think I was five when I had fun with these shucks. Mama had left me in the house while she went outside to help with the evening chores and milking. The house became dark. I saw those slender shuck shreds lying so close to the open hole in the firebox. I picked up a piece that was three or four inches long and touched it to the hot coals nearby. The shuck just smoldered bright red as I stood before the mirror that hung above the small sink in the corner of the kitchen and swirled my hand around making lighted circles. The shuck did not blaze but just smoldered then died. That was fun—until Mama came into the house after she had finished milking and discovered my entertainment. She scolded me severely, lit the lamp, and said, "I left you inside in the warm but you didn't appreciate that. From now on, you'll go outside in the bitter cold with me when I do my chores." And I did.

The two metal lids on the stovetop nearest the left side of the stove were over the firebox. This was the hottest part of the stovetop, and the part of the stove where Mama did the cooking. The two lids over the oven were for simmering, while the two to the right kept food warm.

Corncobs, "prairie chips," wood scraps, or any burnable fuel that was available filled the fuel box that sat beside the range. Mama and I often gathered "prairie chips" for summer time cooking, especially when the corncob supply was low. These chips were dried dung left by the cattle in the pasture. They made a quick, hot fire, and left volumes of ashes. The wood was scraps left from building projects, and rotted off fence posts. Few trees grew here. Coal, which was expensive, was our winter heating fuel.

Above the fuel box, small metal black kitchen match holder hung on the wall. This holder held a regular sized box of kitchen matches.

A supply of warm water for washing hands was always available in the large water reservoir at the left side of the kitchen range.

Below this reservoir was the "slop" bucket. The "slop" for the hogs contained potato and other vegetable peelings that mama cooked, the small quantity of water used to rinse the gravy skillet (gravy was usually prepared for all our meals), skimmed milk, and left over food not given to the dog, cat, or chickens. During the coldest days of winter, mama cooked "hooch" for the hogs. "Hooch" was ground grain that she cooked like corn meal mush. The hogs hungrily fought for a share of the warm food.

Above the cook top of the range was the "warming oven," a space designed to keep food warm until it was served. Mama stored her cast iron skillets here. Iron skillets and an iron Dutch oven were our main cooking utensils. We did have a few white enameled saucepans, too.

Our three flat irons, used for ironing our clothes, were stored on the top of the stove farthest from the firebox where they kept warm but were not hot enough for ironing. We had no place to store them. The removable wooden handles were stored in the cabinet drawer with the dishtowels. When we were ready to iron, these irons were placed on the cook top above the firebox to heat quickly. An iron with the handle attached was used for ironing for a few minutes. Then the iron was returned to the stovetop and the handle attached to another iron which was used until the ironing was done.

In the space directly behind the stove, attached to the wall, was a clothes rack with many prongs, or "arms." This was where we hung the wet clothes to dry in winter.

* * *

The tall metal kitchen stool stood in this area. The legs were originally dark green, but the seat had become shiny metal from much use. Mama often sat on it as she prepared fresh green beans, peeled potatoes and prepared other foods for cooking. That stool was where I sat when Mama combed and braided my hair. I sat on that stool when I did something that displeased Mama. Sitting on that stool was a dreaded punishment because each time Mama walked past me, as she prepared a meal; she addressed negative remarks at me. One of the most common remarks was "You have sinned against God." I came to hate that stool.

* * *

To the right, a small shallow white sink hung on the north wall. The sink drain was connected to a metal barrel (septic tank) buried behind the house. Linen or flour-sack hand towels hung to the left of the sink on the north window frame. My dad's razor strop hung under the towels. To the right of the sink, a window laid on its side. I called it a "lazy window." It slid open to provide convenient access to the water barrel in the water room.

When we were thirsty, we opened this window, reached into the water room for the tin cup that hung on a nail on the window frame inside the water room, dipped it into the fresh water—presto, a cup of fresh, cool water.

No one realized that this common drinking cup and the open barrel of water was the reason colds quickly spread to everyone. We had colds continuously especially during cold weather. In the winter, I constantly had a cold and coughed. The black Smith Brothers or golden-colored Vick's cough drops were always at hand. Oh, how I detested the taste of those cough drops!

A small wall desk with a thick cardboard drop-down writing surface filled the solid half of this window. I kept my special school papers in this desk.

The medicine cabinet with a mirror on the door hung above the sink. Our medicines were stored here. On the second shelf set my dad's shaving mug with the brush, shaving soap, and his straight-edged razor, the common type of razor men used for shaving. One of the medicines kept on the bottom was the camphor gum-turpentine liniment that Mama mixed. (Its uses are described in the "pioneer medicine" story.) The horrible-tasting vermifuge for my "stomach worms" was beside the liniment. Mama said that she gave me the vermifuge beginning in my toddler days because "You grit and grind your teeth at night." (She believed I had worms that were coming up into my throat.) This "worm" treatment continued until I was a teenager.

The narrow shelves to the right side of the medicine cabinet held toiletries. An old-fashioned metal comb pocket, the place for everyone's comb, hung on this wall. Tooth brushes were stored in a cup on the shelf above this comb pocket. My toothbrush was used irregularly; salt and soda was the "tooth paste." Ugh!

* * *

Two steps to the left, the golden-oak finished kitchen cabinet was between the two long north windows. The zinc-covered counter of this cabinet was a pullout worktable that we did not pull out because crockery bowls were stored on it. Several 25-pound tin cans with lids sat on the floor next to this cabinet in front of the window. Mama kept dried corn, beans and peas in these cans.

Inside the top of the cabinet, on the left, was the flour storage bin with a flour sifter at the bottom. I think the bin held 10 pounds of flour. One could sift the flour into the oval-shaped metal pan that set beneath the sifter, then remove the pan of sifted flour to the table, and with the tin flour scoop fill a coffee cup (we did not have a special measuring cup) to make a cake or take handfuls of the flour for making bread. A large uncovered rectangular-shaped molded heavy glass salt dish sat at the other end of this space. Salt and pepper shakers, and small jars of spices, set between the flour pan and salt dish. This area was rarely neat. However, slatted doors at the sides could be pulled together to conceal this compartment. Two short doors concealed two shelves above this area. On these shelves were stored extracts, food coloring, coffee,

Mama's golden oak kitchen cabinet "The Hoosier Cabinet" was made in New Castle, Indiana..

cocoa, and other miscellaneous items. Many small flat paper items were stacked to the ceiling on top of the cabinet.

Below the pull out work table was a large door that concealed our pots and pans. A wire rack, attached inside of the door, held the various-sized flat aluminum pan lids. Mama's cast iron skillets and enameled pans did not have matching lids.

Three storage drawers were on the right hand side below the zinc worktable. The bottom drawer, the largest, was the breadbox perfect for homemade bread. The breadboard, used for kneading bread and rolling out piecrusts and cookies, was stored beneath the pullout work table. Below the breadboard was a shallow drawer for dishtowels. (In 1982, I showed my co-workers at Soil Conservation Office in New Castle, Indiana, a picture of this cabinet, as it set in the yard with the other furniture from Mama's house ready for the auction. They said, "That cabinet was the 'Hoosier Cabinet' and was manufactured in New Castle, Indiana.") That surprised me.

* * *

Another step to the left was the dining area furnished with an old cherry drop-leaf table. A colorful floral-designed oilcloth covered the table. We kept our largest kerosene lamp on the table. It had red and yellow hand-painted flowers on the glass base. The lamp chimney was plain clear glass. Kerosene lamps were our only light source at night, and in the dark days of winter. This light was yellowish in color. (Another lamp that was popular at that time was the Aladdin lamp. The fuel for this lamp was white gasoline. Instead of a wick, this lamp used a silk mantle on each of the two tubes. It provided a bright white light.) A clear cut-glass sugar bowl with a cut-glass lid (Mama said that this sugar bowl was brought to America from Germany.), a cut-glass spoon holder, and salt and pepper shakers were always at the center of the table. Three straight-backed unmatched wooden chairs and a backless wooden stool were kept around the table.

All our meals were served at this table. When my dad, mama and I ate, the table was smaller with the leaf at the back of the table dropped then the table was half an oval. However, when hired men or my brothers were home, the table was oval-shaped. My dad always sat on the backless chair next to the china cabinet. My place was next to the oak kitchen cabinet. Mama sat next to me. Very limited conversation accompanied our meals. After Mama and I had eaten, we sometimes played dominos (double six set) or a homemade board game called "Fox and Geese." Sadly, I do not recall the design of the playing area of board or the rules. A black button represented the "fox" and white buttons the "geese."

Some of my favorite foods included baked chicken with dressing, homemade noodles, fresh creamed corn, homemade bread, homemade dill pickles, kraut that I helped make and kraut cobbler. A favorite dish was kraut cobbler that Mama made using sour kraut, flour, sugar, and cinnamon mixed together then baked in a pie curst lined baking dish. Mama had no recipe and I have been unable to duplicate it from memory.

* * *

One winter evening after everyone else had retired, I completed my task, and was ready to go to bed. I quickly grasped the lamp chimney to "blow out" the fire on the burning wick. Wow! That hot chimney burned my right hand! I quickly set that chimney back on the lamp, then immediately ran to the sink and plopped my hand into the cool dirty wash water in the white enameled wash pan. In just a few minutes, the burning was gone. When morning came, there was not a trace of the burn on my hand. I knew I should not grasp the hot chimney, but I was too tired to think. Why did I go to the cold water with my burning hand? I have no idea, as we never used cool water to ease pain of a burn.

* * *

A dark walnut-finished china cabinet filled the corner along the west wall. The collection of dishes on the paper-lined shelves was visible through the two long glass inserts in the doors. Colorful flower-edged shelf paper brightened the gloomy corner. Below these doors were two drawers—our flatware was stored in one drawer and miscellaneous kitchen supplies were in the other. Short solid wooden doors at the bottom of the cabinet concealed two shelves, which was a safe place to store pies, cakes, cookies or other food items.

* * *

Our catalogues were stacked to the ceiling on top, and on the floor below the china cabinet. The Sears Roebuck and Montgomery Ward catalogs always fascinated me as I looked through them and dreamed. Catalog shopping brought stores conveniently into our kitchen, and we were regular catalog shoppers. It was convenient to sit at home, search through the catalogs, send an order, and include the payment in cash. Our mail carrier delivered the order to our house, or left it by our mailbox. Catalogue shopping eliminated the need to make long tiring shopping trips to Benkelman, Nebraska (25 miles one-way). In addition, more choices were available through the catalogs than in the small stores in Benkelman, the county seat and largest town in Dundy County, Nebraska.

I recall one Christmas; Mama had made some candy before Christmas. It was stored in a tin canister on top of the china cabinet. I do not recall why our rat terrier farm dog was in the house as this was most unusual. Mama went outside to work. I wanted some of that candy and quickly took some from the tin canister. Just as I was retuning the canister to the top of the cabinet, I heard Mama coming. I had not had time to eat the candy, so I quickly hid that "stolen" candy in the bottom of the china cabinet. When Mama came into the kitchen, the dog pointed with his nose to the bottom of the china cabinet. Fortunately, Mama never understood his "pointing." Candy was the Christmas treat. Gifts were not given or exchanged.

On the west wall, to the left of the china cabinet, hung an old-fashioned crank telephone. When I questioned Mama why the phone was not connected, she said that it was connected to the phone line at the end of our lane until one Halloween night. Uncle Andy, her brother, phoned and said "Boo" then hung up. Mama continued saying that she recognized his distinctly accented voice, and was angry. She cancelled the telephone service immediately. (Mama said that barbed wire fences sometimes served as telephone lines before regular telephone lines were available.)

In the mid 1930's, a small wooden chest of drawers sat below the telephone. On this chest was a small radio that was powered by a car battery. When the car was needed, the battery was replaced in the car. We used the radio just for newscasts. A few times Mama allowed me to listen to the radio while my dad was out in the field, but it was always off before he came into the house. I do not know whether he would have been angry if we listened to the radio, or not. Mama was always afraid that using the radio would weaken the battery so much that it would not start the car. If that had happened, then my dad would have roared at us. Mama always insisted that both of us had to be busy working when he was in the house.

Next on this west wall, a black Kenmore foot-pedal sewing machine was located in front of the west window. I learned to sew on this machine when I was seven years old. I hemmed sugar sacks for dishtowels. Sugar was sold in 50 and 100-pound bags made of a white cotton cloth. These sacks made absorbent lint-free dishtowels. I never made doll clothes, because I had no dolls. This west window provided light for sewing during the daytime.

I begged to sew all of the time, but Mama had nothing for me to sew. I even wanted to make a quilt but she said that making a quilt would not be profitable. Garments for adults were made into children's clothes. Often coats and jackets were ripped apart, the fabric was turned inside out to hide faded or worm spots, and then sewn back together for a "new" garment. Pioneers did with whatever they had instead of buying new.

Mama had a yard of medium-blue fabric with small, rose-colored flowers left after she made herself a dress. (The fabric had been a Christmas gift to Mama from Alvin, my brother.) I did not want that fabric lying around, to me that seemed like a waste especially when I wanted to sew. I begged and begged until she bought a yard of plain pink fabric to use with the blue for a dress. We ordered a pattern from the *Capper's Weekly* newspaper for ten cents. I never read the confusing pattern directions. Mama did not understand them either. I designed the color-block dress using the shirtwaist pattern with gored skirt. As I used the pattern pieces, I made each half of the bodice of each color sewn together with vertical seams. I did the same with the sleeves and collar. The gores of the skirt were alternated blue print and plain pink. In finishing, I made the buttonholes by hand.

What a delight! I was just 12 years old and I constructed the dress I had "seen in my mind!" Nevertheless, I could only wear it at home. How I wanted to wear it to school! Mama called it that "old patched up thing." Our farm dog liked to jump up on people, a bad habit we were unable to break. His claws scraped down the front of my dress and soon ruined it. My dress was often mended, patched and patched. So sad!

Above the sewing machine beside the window frame attached to the wall, was a brass bracket that held a clear squat-type glass base kerosene lamp with a clear glass chimney. This lamp provided light for sewing in the evenings, or on cloudy days.

To the left in the last corner of the kitchen—excuse me—in the living room portion of the room, a wind-up phonograph occupied space on a small rectangular table. The playing arm of this phonograph had a heavy round head attached to a double curved swiveled arm. The needles were replaced after playing only a few records. I had to be careful not to drop the head on the record as it lay on the turntable because the needles could scratch or break the records. The 78-rpm records were stored on the shelf below the tabletop. Among the titles were: *The Old Rugged Cross, Hand Me Down My Walking Cane*, De *Campton Races, Dem Golden Slippers, Spring Time in the Rockies,* and *Two Black Crows*, a slap-stick comedy. I played these records repeatedly, and often sang with them.

Mama's large harmonica and my small harmonica were on the shelf beside the records. Sometimes we would both play our harmonicas together. Mama loved to sing two songs *The East Bound Train Was Crowded* and the *Little Black Mustache* that she had learned in her younger days. We did not have music for these songs.

Our newspapers were *The Benkelman Post* (a weekly), and the *Capper's Weekly.* Also, two magazines, *The Nebraska Farmer*, and *Successful Farmer,* (both once a month), and Mama's "spiritualism" newspapers were kept in the magazine rack beside the rocking chair. The only book was a children's book *Things To Do* (an activity book) that had been given to my brothers and me, a Christmas gift 1928-29 (as inscribed inside the book). This book contained directions to make simple things like dollhouse furniture from cardboard, a "buzz-saw" using string and a button, a cigar box banjo, and other simple toys and a small book, *Memories,* written by my Aunt Alma Simmons. In it, she told of living in a sod house. She described the heartache of mud from the leaking roof when it rained and of her many escapades of running away from her home to her relatives who lived on nearby farms.

This rocker was nice place to sit or nap. I napped there many nights in the fall while I waited for everyone to finish eating supper (our evening meal) during my grade school days. I was so hungry that I would "wolf" down my food. Mama said, "You must help with the dishes before you go to bed." Rising at five a.m., I was exhausted by ten p.m. I was so tired that I fell asleep in this rocker.

Mama cleared the table, washed the dishes, and went to bed. Hours after everyone else had retired, I wakened shivering in the cold kitchen as the fire was out in the stove. I undressed and went to bed. I awakened Mama (maybe she was not asleep, I do not know), as I crawled into bed from the foot to my space next to the wall. She always greeted my entrance with a sneer, "Were you sitting up with the hired men (the corn huskers)?" That made me unhappy, NO! That made me angry! I was so tired that I just could not stay awake. I did not appreciate her remarks, but I could not protest. I was just a little girl.

A seven-day green "marbled" mantel clock was on a shelf above this small table. My dad had purchased the clock for $27.00 before he was married. He had a special small key to wind it every week. The tuneful bell sounded on the hour and on the half hour. We missed hearing the melodic bell when the clock ran down as then the house was very quiet.

Mama chose colorful floral-designed wallpaper that required no matching for the walls of this multi-purpose room. The ceiling paper with an all-over design-on-design was white, or off white. The kitchen range frequently smoked; soon the white ceiling paper became dark from the smoke.

When I was around the age of seven or eight, I helped with the papering. It was fun to use the wallpaper paste brush to "paint" the back side of the paper with cooked paste made with flour, a bit of lye (to discourage moths), and water. After I pasted the paper, Mama held the long strips of wet pasted paper (pasted sides together) draped across one arm, then with a special dry wallpaper brush in her other hand pressed the wet paper onto the wall. She always made sure the seams (where the strips of paper over-lapped) were pressed flat. Then my job was to take a two-inch wide wooden roller, and roll each seam smooth. If any paste oozed out, I wiped it off with a clean dry rag. A newly papered room always gave a satisfying lift with the fresh clean smell and clear bright colors. I loved the fresh aroma of a "just papered room."

Window shades and floral-designed sheer curtains hung at each of the three tall windows. When I was a freshman in high school, Mama used two of the sheer curtains to make me a formal for a Valentine party. First, Mama washed and ironed the curtains. Then she sewed the top of the curtains together leaving an opening large enough for my head. Next, she stitched together the side seams of the curtains below an opening left for each of my arms. The hem of the dress was the original hem of the curtains. She asked me to cut out two medium-sized red construction paper hearts, and several smaller red hearts. She attached a medium sized heart on each shoulder of the dress, and smaller paper hearts that were attached as a border near the hem of the dress. We purchased a pink bias-cut satin nightgown at Ireland's Dry Goods store in Benkelman for one dollar that I used for my slip. I had a red ribbon sash. Mama was proud of her creation, but it hardly fit in with the gowns the other girls wore. After the party, we ripped the dress apart and returned the curtains to the windows. The dress cost nothing. We made do with the materials we had.

* * *

Open the solid wooden door and view a room with green calcimined walls and a painted brown wooden floor—the bedroom. One tall window was on the west side of the room and another one on the south side of the room. A green window shade and a plain white sheer curtain hung at each window. The two double beds were along the outside wall. A long floor-to-ceiling built-in closet was on the inside wall. My parents slept in the first bed.

I remember sleeping between my parents. I awakened one cold, winter night—much, much too warm. I squirmed and squirmed and kicked until I awakened Mama (she slept next to the wall). She asked me what was wrong. I whined, "I'm too hot!" as I squirmed again. This was my very first memory; I probably was not more than two years old.

Mama rose up, and pushed me over against the wall and said, "Now, if you git cold just shut up and git to sleep!" I did. Oh, how great the coolness of the nearby frosty wall felt!

My two older brothers, Alvin, and Lyle, slept in the other double bed. The west window was at their head and the south window near their feet. A small dark-walnut finished dresser topped with a small mirror sat in the opposite corner. A white hand-embroidered dresser scarf covered the dresser top. A small kerosene lamp set on the dresser.

(In 1929, my brothers moved to Benkelman, Nebraska to attend high school. Mama built a one-room house with an attached one-car garage on the hill near the high school. She had purchased four lots at a tax sale for $1.25 according to a document I found in her records. My brothers came home on weekends for a year or two. They drove their Ford coupe to and from school.

Alvin, my older brother, graduated in 1933, but Lyle became absorbed in trucking. They visited frequently, but never lived at home after 1930.)

Lyle and Alvin stand beside their Ford coupe. This car provided their transportation to high school.

* * *

17

Now back to the bedroom. A flue was in the wall opposite the beds. A round metal cover with a pretty scenery picture hid the flue opening. I never recall seeing a stove here, but I remember Mama talking about a stove in the bedroom. In the 1930's, a large bin with a wooden frame made of 2x2 inch wood was attached to the wooden floor of this bin. Our winter supply of food—100 pound sacks of flour, 50 pound sacks of sugar, bags of corn meal, gallon pails of Karo syrup, honey, and sorghum were in the bin. The bin was mouse-free storage. The box contents were hidden behind a curtain of colorful printed flour or feed sacks that were attached to the wooden frame.

The long built-in floor to ceiling closet, the only closet in the house, was in the corner nearest the kitchen. Our clothes hung on hooks. Mama insisted that I had to crawl to the back of the closet to get clothes she wanted. I hated this task as my hair in long braids curled around my head usually caught on the hooks. The rarely used garments were always at the back. The shelf, above the hooks for the clothes, made an excellent storage place for blankets, quilts, and feather beds.

Sleeping under, and between feather beds was wonderful. A feather bed, a quilt-sized "pillow" filled with feathers, was a very light-weight cover. I loved to sleep between feather beds in winter. When a feather bed served as mattress, it was snuggly cozy and warm. One could not lie "on" a feather bed as the smallest fluffiest chicken feathers filled the blue and white stripped ticking. The feathers let the body "sink" to the surface below, yet provided warmth without weight. Goose feathers, when available, made the lightest fluffiest feather beds. Our pillows were filled with chicken feathers.

However, the mattresses on the beds in the bedroom were "shuck ticks." Each fall the "blue and white striped shuck ticks" were taken outside, ripped open, emptied, washed, and then filled with fresh shucks after the corn had been shelled. These mattresses remained light and puffy for several weeks after they were filled with fresh corn shucks. New shucks released a relaxing aroma in the room.

After my brothers had left home, my dad could not husk all the corn by hand alone. Homeless men roamed the country; most of them had only a change of clothes, a blanket, a horse, and a rifle. They would stop and work on a farm doing whatever work was available. These were our "hired hands." They received room and board, both for themselves and for their horse. In addition, their clothes were laundered without charge. During harvest season, they earned a wage. These hired "hands" always shared the bedroom with my dad, and slept in my brothers' former bed. I believe this was the when Mama and I began sleeping on the day bed in the front room. I was probably five years old at this time.

One man, "Windy," came regularly every fall near the end of harvest for several years, and stayed during the winter. He helped with the chores and other tasks. Then Mama and I had fewer chores to do. He was friendly and helpful, and he loved to "spin tales." ("Spinning" tales was the reason for his nickname; we never knew his real name.) If there was no work, he would go hunting for jack rabbits or pheasants for the table.

A few steps to another wooden door. Stop! Look up! Above the door frame, a 22 repeating Remington rifle hung on two spike nails. When I was in my late teens, I took this rifle, picked up shells stored on the top shelf in the water room, and went rabbit hunting. I sauntered around to the back of the chicken house near the barbed wire pasture fence. I thought I saw something. I stopped—was it an eye? Or an ear? Or just a flick of a sagebrush branch? I watched then chanced a shot. Sure enough, I had hit a rabbit in the head. With beginner's luck of a perfect record, I returned the rife to its resting place and retired from rabbit hunting.

Above this door, the "scuttle hole," the access door to the attic was located. A ladder was brought into the house to enter the attic; therefore, nothing was ever stored there except a metal wind-up train that belonged to my brothers. I recalled seeing that train once and knew it was stored in the attic. I begged and begged to play with it, but the answer was always the same: "No, that belongs to your brothers." Mama gave it to my brother, Lyle after he was married.

* * *

Open the wooden door and enter into the front room. This room was rarely used until Mama and I began to sleep on the day bed, which could be made up into a "couch." A large three-drawer dark walnut-finished dresser, topped with a white scarf and a kerosene lamp, was in the opposite corner of the room from the daybed.

A dark-walnut recliner with black leather upholstery set in front of the dresser. The recliner had a foot rest, and was designed similar to today's recliners. The back could be adjusted by raising or lowering a metal rod into the notches in the wooden rail at the back of the chair for the desired recline. The front of the chair had a footrest that we extended for the desired recline. It was a comfortable chair.

A thirty-six inch-inch square oak library table was between the recliner and our bed. A large ruffled hand-crocheted pineapple-design doily covered the tabletop. (I have this doily in a reed circular frame hanging on the wall behind my TV.) A small dark reed-sewing basket trimmed with light tan and white seashells, a gift to me from my Grandpa Grams, was in the center. (I still have this, my first sewing basket.) Sometimes Mama's Bible would be on the table. The small shelf below was dust covered.

The foot-pedal pump parlor organ in the corner was near the door that opened into the kitchen. Mama said, "This organ was brought by a covered wagon to Nebraska from Maryland. The beautifully carved top with mirrors was left behind because it would not fit in the wagon." The bellows and some of the reeds needed repair. She devised a way to seal the billows, or air-reserve bag, and straighten the reeds. It was playable and sounded in tune. Several song books were on the organ. I learned to read music and played with my right hand, and sometimes improvised for the left hand, or played "by ear" as I sang.

The dark walnut finished round top organ stool, protected with a white popcorn-stitch hand-crocheted cover, sat in front of the organ. (This hand crocheted cover attached to a large circular frame decorates my living room wall today.) It was fun to sit on the stool, and twirl and twirl—when no one was watching. The ornately hand-carved legs were finished with a decorated metal sleeve that ended with claw feet grasping a clear glass ball.

* * *

A shelf, above the organ held knick-knacks, and a tall glass vase that was filled with colorful crepe paper flowers. I loved to make new flowers when the old ones became faded and dusty. Roses, red roses my favorite, were the easiest to make. Beside the vase of paper flowers stood a photo of Mama's father, Mike Grams, a homesteader. Next to it was my brother, Alvin's 1933 high school graduation picture. Also, on the shelf with the pictures were a gold and white china shoe that that been broken. Mama had mended it with "white lead." A minute-sized blue and white china shoe, my favorite, was beside the gold and white shoe. The tiny, turned-up toe of that blue and white shoe was adorned with a miniature white rose bud. How I admired that shoe! I tried to stretch it one day. Results? Too sad to write about.

A small black heating stove was connected with a black stovepipe to the flue. The stove was rarely used, even in winter. The only room regularly heated was the kitchen. Our rare baths, especially in winter, were taken in the evening in the kitchen in front of the open oven door. A blanket or sheet draped over the backs of the straight-backed chairs provided a bit of privacy. In the summer, this heating stove was disconnected from the flue, and set against the wall. When in use the stove sat on a "stove board," a 36-inch square of lightweight wood covered with metal, to catch sparks that fell from the firebox. The stove board prevented damage to the floor from the sparks. A coal bucket with paper, cobs, and a poker were kept beside the stove.

Colorful floral-designed wallpaper covered the walls were finished with a matching wide floral border at the top of the walls. Hanging on the walls were portraits of Mama's family in huge ornate gold frames. I remember the large oval-shaped framed photo of Aunt Emma, Mama's little sister (who died at the age of 12 at the hands of their cruel uncle, Jacob Wentland); a picture of Grandpa Grams, Mama's father; and Uncle Charlie, Mama's brother, proudly wearing his WWI uniform. Mama said that her mother, Eva would not have her picture taken.

Hand crocheted white lace curtains hung at the glass upper-half panel of the outside front door, and the door to the kitchen. (A hand crocheted glass door curtain stretched in a wooden frame decorates my living room wall.) A shade and a sheer curtain hung at the tall east window. The floor covering was a colorful floral-designed linoleum rug with a wide floral border. The wooden floor around the linoleum was painted dark brown.

*   *   *

The photo on the cover of this book is the farm, which my parents purchased in 1911. It shows a two-roomed gabled-roof frame house with clapboard wooden siding and wooden shingles. The shed-roof addition was built on the north side. This addition became the kitchen-dining-living room and the water room. I do not know when this addition was built. However, I do recall when I was very young that I was on the roof, (I think with my dad) and helped drive nails into the shingled roof. Inside, a wooden clapboard-sided wall was visible in the water room on the side where our chore clothes hung.

Lightning rods adorned each end of the gabled roof (not visible in the photo). Braided copper cables attached to each of the rods that ran across the roof then to the ground on each side of the house ending with rods that were driven into the ground. The lightning rods protected the building from lightning strikes during our frequent severe thunder and lightning storms of summer. Farmers who had two-story barns also used lightning rods for protection.

This was a view of the east side of the house where I was born. The window was in the front room. The attic window was above. The low porch was below the door that opened into the water room. Trees were Chinese elms.

MY FAMILY

My family consisted of my father, my mother, two older brothers, Alvin and Lyle, and myself. Alvin was about 12 years older than I, and Lyle, about 10 years older than I was.

Ellis Blamford Mendenhall, my father, was born in 1881 in a sod house on his father's homestead, near Norton, Kansas. He had two younger sisters, Alma and Lulu. He attended school in a one-room school and finished the eighth grade. However, he did not receive his diploma. He said, "Another boy had done some mischief then blamed me." He continued, "If I'd gone back for my diploma, I'd had to 'take a beating' for that mischief. I was not guilty, and I refused to return for the undeserved punishment."

His family lived in Kansas for several years, and then they moved to Corning, Iowa in 1898. My dad suffered from asthma. The pollen and dampness in Iowa caused him severe breathing problems. Five years later, he decided to "work his way" to California and began to work and travel westward.

He arrived in Dundy County, Nebraska in 1903, and began to work on the farms. Here he found the semi-arid climate favorable to his health. He staked a claim about four miles west of the little village of Rollwitz, Nebraska. However, the best land available through the Homestead Act had been claimed. The soil on his claim was very sandy and suitable only for grazing. Soon after he and my mother were married in 1910, they sold the homestead, and purchased a farm about four miles east of Rollwitz. Andy Grams, Mama's brother, a land broker, had obtained ownership of this farm, which had been someone's homestead a few years earlier.

* * *

Lydia Grams, my mother, was born in Salisbury, Missouri in 1891. Her mother passed away when Mama was just three and half years old. Her father, Mike Grams (my grandpa) was left with a family of four daughters and two sons. He sent his oldest daughter, Matilda, (Aunt May) to Canada to live with relatives. Susan, age seven and a half, Lydia, my mama, age three and a half, and baby Emma, six months old were sent to live with their Aunt Caroline (their mother's sister) and her husband, Uncle Jacob Wentland in Carrington, North Dakota. Grandpa's two sons remained with him. Later, he moved to Dundy County Nebraska and staked a claim for a homestead. In 1902, he applied for citizenship, a requirement of the Homestead Act.

Uncle Jacob and Aunt Caroline had no children. He was very cruel and abusive to my mama. He chose Mama to herd over 100 head of cattle on the open range on foot. He frequently whipped her with a horsewhip whenever she did anything that displeased him. He even threw a pitchfork at her. It hit her in the head and left several scars. Later, he found a gentle riding horse for her. She never attended school in North Dakota.

After eight or nine years, Mama's, sister Susan, slipped a note to their dad, Mike Grams (my grandpa) telling him of the abuse inflicted on my mama. Grandpa came for Mama and found her thinly clad out in a raging blizzard, herding cattle. Grandpa took her from the horse and put her in his wagon, took off his over coat and put it around her. Then he went to Uncle Jacob and asked, "How could he (Uncle Jacob) expect that girl to keep warm in that blizzard in those thin clothes when I (Mike Grams) could not keep warm wearing an overcoat?" He took my mama with him to his homestead in Nebraska. Aunt Susan went to Minneapolis, Minnesota where she worked and attended a Seventh Day Adventist School. Aunt Emma stayed with her aunt and uncle. A few years later Emma, 12 years old (1905), while herding cattle accidentally rode her horse into a slough. The horse was stuck. Emma was cruelly whipped. She died from her injuries. The location of her grave is unknown.

Information in the 1900 census noted that my mama, age nine, attended school—instead she was herding cattle. She began attending school after her father, Mike Grams, brought her to his Nebraska homestead. She became the cook and housekeeper for her father and two brothers, and attended school. She said that she never got past the third grade.

Family photo taken May 1943, standing--
Elsieferne (Author) and her brother, Alvin. Their
parents-- Ellis and Lydia Mendenhall are seated.
The inset picture is Lyle (deceased when this
photo was taken.)

CHAPTER II

FARM BUILDINGS and ANIMAL HOMES

Our tour begins with buildings used for storing feed for the farm animals. Southeast of the farmhouse were two wooden grain bins with tin roofs—one bin built for the storage of ear corn, had slatted-wooden walls that allowed circulation of air through the ear corn. The other had solid walls for the storage of shelled corn, ground grain, and commercial feed for the livestock. The cows loved the molasses-flavored supplement cubes. (The molasses aroma attracted me to sample the cubes, too. They were delicious. Even the older boys confessed at school about eating these yummy-tasting cubes.) The space between these grain bins provided storage place for the farm truck, a Model A Ford. The tin roof of the grain bins extended upwards and formed a gabled roof that covered this space. A big wooden door hung on roller tracks at each end of the both bins. Both doors were opened for full access to either bin.

When Dad needed ground feed for the livestock, he would shovel shelled corn into the bed of the truck, and drove to the Justus Feed Mill in Benkelman. Here the corn was ground, mixed with the appropriate supplement, and bagged. These bags or sacks were made of burlap, a lightweight canvas, and later printed cotton fabrics. These prepared feeds were stored in the enclosed granary.

When I was very young, I remember Mama's large garden south and west of the granaries. An underground water line from the stock tank provided water for the garden. She grew large and small red and yellow tomatoes, potatoes, sweet potatoes, green beans, pole beans, peas, tuber artichokes, parsnips, cabbage, cucumbers, watermelons, cantaloupes, leaf lettuce, carrots, radishes, onions, ground cherries, squash, pumpkins and more. The luscious deep purple huckleberries were a favorite of mine. Yum! Yum!

In addition, Mama had rhubarb in the small fenced-in garden next to the windmill. Within this small fenced in garden, in addition to other vegetables that she grew here were horseradish, a grapevine, and a cherry tree.

Horseradish was a popular seasoning. In fall, we dug the horseradish roots. I helped prepare the roots for eating when I was old enough. Oh, how my eyes burned and tears rolled with each stroke of the scrub brush across those roots. More tears flowed as I ground the roots using the hand-operated food grinder. The hot burning taste of that horseradish, in my opinion was horrible, but my brothers loved it! Probably just to tease me.

* * *

Alvin and Lyle studied the latest methods of raising hogs in their agriculture classes in high school. Soon this big garden space became a pig pen for purebred black and white Hampshire hogs. I loved to watch those clean white-belted baby piglets with their sharp pointed white ears suckle. Red portable A-type hog houses dotted the space along with several self-feeders. These self-feeders were small upright bins that were filled with commercial feed and ground corn. Troughs on each side were covered with iron lids designed for the hogs to lift. These lids protected the feed from the weather. The hogs ate day and night. Bang! Bang! Bang! All of the time. What a tune for sleeping! The former garden water line provided water for the hogs. The feed provided for these hogs was grains, supplement and water.

After my brothers sold their Hampshire hogs, Mama used the A-type houses for her chickens. When I was eight, I contracted pink eye at school, and had to stay home until my eyes were well. The weather was a clear hot spring day, a perfect time to disinfect these houses. Mama asked me to operate our primitive pressure pump that we set inside a bucket. A bracket fit over the outside of the bucket ended with a flat surface was placed on the ground. The operator placed a foot on the flat part of the lever to secure the pump. I was the operator.

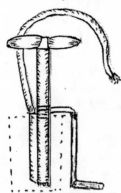

The antique sprayer the Author was using when it exploded showering her with strong disinfectant. (Sketch by the Author)

Mama mixed the concentrated dip disinfectant with water and poured the solution into the sprayer bucket. She held the hose with the nozzle end and sprayed the inside of the A-type houses, while I energetically pumped with all my strength to keep up the pressure—when boom! The hose blew off the pump; dip solution blasted me! I screamed; my face, arms and eyes were burning! We rushed to the house. Manna poured cold water over my face and arms and rinsed out my eyes, a difficult task. My eyes were cured of pink eye. I returned to school the next day.

* * *

A grinder, (a sweep mill) located in front of the granaries was used to grind corn. This grinder was powered by one horse as it walked in a circle around the grinder. I was very young and do not recall exactly how this was all arranged, but I can clearly "see" the circular path worn by the horse as it walked around and around the mill.

Later, this mill disappeared and portable corncribs with woven wire sides were built in this area. Additional farmland was purchased and that meant more storage was needed for the ear corn. It was very important to keep the corn out of the sand. If we had a bumper crop, sometimes it became necessary to pile the ear corn on the ground. Mama objected to the corn lying on the sand. However, many of our neighbors piled their corn on the ground.

* * *

Dad kept his Poland China hogs in a large fenced area, east of the two wooden grain storage bins. He built a large hog house with a cement floor. Hogs love to root even though every pig, when it was several weeks old, had a small brass wire ring clipped into its nose. The purpose of these rings was to discourage rooting. Nothing appeared to discourage a hog from rooting. During the dust bowl days, big holes were rooted in the ground at each end of this hog house making it difficult for the hogs to enter. Chickens had no problems flying into the hog house and laying their eggs on the floor, but I had a problem getting into the hog house to check for eggs.

These hogs were fed the "slop" from the kitchen and grain in metal troughs made from 30 or 50-gallon metal tanks from old water heaters cut in half. One of the troughs was reserved for water. An underground water line from the large stock tank provided fresh drinking water for these animals and with plenty of water for their favorite activity—rolling in a water hole.

The stock tank was next to the hog lot, and was accessible both from the barnyard and inside the horse corral for all the livestock in the pasture.

The horse corral was near the flat wooden-sided horse barn or stable. Inside the barn were four large stalls; two horses occupied each stall. The horses were secured in their stalls with a rope attached with a snap in the ring of the halter that each horse wore. The harness hung on the south wall, the only side of the barn with entrance doors. The manger, filled with hay, was at the front of each stall. At the each end of a manager, each horse had a feed box for the morning and evening oats and corn. During the summer, the work horses usually spent the night outside in the corral where it was cooler.

The barn was built with flat eight or ten-inch wide boards pounded tightly together then nailed securely to the wooden framework of the barn. The gabled roof had the same type of construction and was not shingled. The barn doors constructed with flat wooden boards were braced securely on the inside. Metal hinges secured the doors to the barn.

The corn and oats for feed were stored in a large wooden box inside the southeast corner of the barn. Hay was stored in two long stacks north of the barn. It was convenient to put the hay into the mangers through long narrow horizontal doors on the north side of the barn. These doors were kept open during the summer, and closed in the winter except when the mangers were filled. Many times, I filled the mangers with hay, but I was never allowed in the barn with the horses.

The milk cows were kept the barbed-wire corral near the milking barn. The "cow barn," as we called it, had stalls for eight cows. The cows were tied in the stalls with a rope around their neck attached to the top manger rail. The mangers were filled with hay. Mornings and evenings, we gave each cow a portion of grain and supplement in the wooden feed box at each end of the manger. The feed storage box was inside at the south side of the barn.

Alvin with a colt in 1929 standing in front of the horse barn.

The construction of the cow barn was the same as the horse barn except the cow barn had a shed roof. In the summer, we usually did the milking outside in the corral where it was cooler. The milk cows remained outside in the corral all night (this kept the barn cleaner and saved work). During the coldest weather, the cows stayed inside the barn during the night. The barns were cleaned every morning. The "cleanings" (manure) were piled outside the barn not far from the largest door.

The summer I was six years old, I learned to help with the milking. I went to sleep many times at night as I sat beside Bessie, my gentle milk cow. My hands and arms would just fall to my sides, as my eyes closed against my will. Gentle Bessie walked away, and left me sitting on my one-legged milk stool with the milk pail clutched between my knees.

I was never permitted to walk in the pasture to bring the cows home for milking. My dad walked to get the cows after he came home after a long day's work in the field. We had no riding horse. We milked the cows after supper. It was very late before bedtime arrived. I was exhausted.

* * *

A long shed with a metal roof formed part of this corral. The three sides, covered with metal sheeting, provided the cattle with shelter against the cold winter wind and snow. I recall one year my dad roped a young steer and tied it to one of the support posts of the open side of this shed before he came into house. I do not recall why he had tied up the steer, "maybe the steer had crawled through the fence and my dad was going to teach him a lesson." Mama and I were shredding cabbage to make kraut. He suddenly thought it was necessary to supervise us in the kraut making.

After he returned to his work outside, he discovered that he had stayed in the house too long. The steer had run around and around the post until he choked himself to death. Was my dad angry when he saw the dead steer! Mama said, "You should have taken care of your work instead of sticking your nose in my business. I have made kraut for years and did not need your meddling." That was the only year we had beef to eat.

West of the cow barn was a small metal-covered shed and a pen for the baby calves that were weaned from their mothers. Mama and I taught these calves to drink milk from a bucket. The trick was to dip your hand into the bucket of warm milk, and then force the calf to open its mouth for a taste of the milk before all of the milk dripped off the finger. I used my middle finger in the mouth of the calf as I pushed its head down into the bucket. The natural posture for nursing was for the calf to reach up. Several attempts were required for a calf to learn to suck the milk with its head down and not get the milk in its nose. Often the calf would bite down hard on the finger that was in its mouth. How that hurt! Happy tail switching resulted once that hungry baby learned where to find the milk. When the calves wanted more milk, they would "butt" the bucket from our hands. "Butting" was the natural way to get every drop of milk from the mama cow's udder. We usually had six to eight calves to bucket feed two times a day. We always kept fresh hay for them. What a relief it was when the calves and cows quit bawling for each other! This bawling was heard for miles, especially in the early morning when everything else was calm and quiet.

More prairie hay was stacked behind the cow barn. It was easy to throw hay from this stack into the corral for the cows. In addition to the haystack, farm machinery was parked in this area. The old unused horse-drawn machinery was with the machines that were used every year. The old machines were kept because sometimes a part from these machines could be used to replace a broken part on a newer machine. Nothing was thrown away.

* * *

Nearby was the two-room house my dad built on his homestead. (In the 1908 photo of his homestead, this was the house on the hill away from the barn.) He moved the two-room clapboard-sided wooden frame building with wood shingles on the gabled roof to this farm. Later he converted it into a car shed. To do this, he removed the siding from the south end of the house, and used this siding to make two big entrance doors. Iron hinges attached these doors to the building. This small house became a nice car-shed (garage) for our Model T touring car. Our winter supply of cobs was protected from the weather in a large bin in the east side of the building.

Later, my dad bought the 1933 V-8 4-door Ford car, unbeknown to Mama. When he drove it home, she screamed at him. His reason for buying a different car was that he hated to start the Model T because the starter was a hand crank. (This was before cars had batteries and self-starters.) This Ford V-8 had an electric starter and was a very dependable car. (I drove this car when I obtained my drivers' license. It provided my transportation until I left Nebraska years later.)

The new car needed a larger car shed. Dad tore the old car shed down, salvaged the lumber, and built a longer larger car shed near the mulberry trees between the house and chicken house. A bin for the corncobs was on the north side of this car shed. One of Mama's objections to a new car was that money had to be borrowed to pay for it. She often said, "We have mortgage upon mortgage." Years later, I reviewed the deeds of the farm after my cousin Harry Grams (son of Mama's brother, Andy) had purchased the farm. These records verified her comments.

I was 14 or 15 when I first attempted to drive this car. I had washed and waxed it near the car-shed door. Then I thought it would be nice to drive it carefully into the shed. I started the engine, held open the front door to make sure that I did not hit the shed wall. I had forgotten that the front doors opened from the front. Yes, the door caught on the shed wall and bent the hinges before I could hit the brake. I was very frightened! A few days later, Lyle was home and Mama asked him to fix that door. He said, "That is no big problem, Sis," as he quickly bent the hinges back into place

* * *

A beautiful cone-shaped 35-40 foot honey locust tree grew beside the original car shed. There were very long thorns on the trunk and branches. Every year an abundant supply of long seed pods matured, but none ever sprouted. Under this tree sat a one-horse buggy where it gradually drifted away into memory. The wooden wheels within the iron rims shrunk more each year. Chickens loved the shade of this majestic tree and roosted in the branches. Tommy, the black farm cat, loved to nap in the box under the spring seat of the old buggy.

* * *

Not far to the left of this tree was my dad's tool shed. It housed the forge and the bellows, iron working and wood working tools (many had been his dad's). However, this shed was neglected until it collapsed. The boards from the shed and the tools lay where they fell. The blacksmith tools included different sized long-handled tongs, the forge and bellows and a variety of sledge hammers. The large and small anvil looked abandoned out in the hot sun and blowing sand.

Blacksmithing skills were needed to maintain a farm in the early 1900's. (The tool shed was just to the right of the house on the cover of this book.) The process to make a needed repair was a hot fire in the forge (special type of coal was used) fanned by air from the bellows, and a piece of iron to be formed into the needed part. The iron held with tongs was thrust into the red-hot coal fire. It soon became red or white-hot. This white hot metal was laid on the anvil and was molded and shaped with blows from a sledge hammer. The metal was heated several times before it was shaped as desired, and then it was quickly dunked into a bucket of cold water to cool it. I was fascinated to watch the metal working process. Hot sparks flew as the hot iron was molded with blows from a sledge hammer into the new shape.

The woodworking tools lying in the sand included—saws, braces and bits for drilling holes in wood, several sizes and styles of hammers, rasps, files, hatchets, a draw knife, planes for smoothing wood, large and small squares (for making things true to size). Other tools included bits for drilling holes in metal, tin snipes, a bench vise, a monkey wrench (an early model of a pipe wrench), pipe wrenches, and more. I picked up the tools and looked at them. I mentioned them to Mama. She said, "Your dad should take care of the tools." Finally, the abandoned tools were taken to safe places. After my dad built the new tool shed in front of the cow barn, the forge and all the other tools were once again in one place. (My grandpa's tin snips survive in my tool collection.)

* * *

The icehouse, west of the tool shed, had cement walls eight feet deep down in the earth. Only a foot of the walls was visible above ground. The gabled wooden-shingled roof came to within a foot of the ground. The tallest visible wall was on the south side. It contained the only opening, a small wooden door. Inside the icehouse below the wooden door, a ladder leaned against this wall just below the door opening. The ladder was made with 2x2 inch wooden rails with flat wood scraps nailed across the rails for the rungs. It provided access to the floor.

During the coldest bone-chilling winter weather, the water in the stock tank froze several inches thick. My brothers and my dad would break the ice in the stock tank with an ax, and then packed the ice in clean hay on the floor.

During the summer, we froze ice cream using ice from our own ice supply. Ice cream was a rare special treat. One July fourth, my brothers used ice from the icehouse to freeze ice cream. They operated the freezer. They packed the crushed ice, layered with rock salt around the metal ice cream canister (The liquid ice cream mixture was inside this metal canister.) This metal canister set inside the wooden bucket. An iron dome-shaped cap that covered the top of the ice cream canister was attached to a hook on each side of this wooden bucket. Metal gears inside the dome cap meshed with the gears on the canister lid when the handle was turned and the paddles inside the canister scraped the frozen mixture constantly off the walls of the canister. My brothers turned the handle to freeze the ice cream mixture. I watched them impatiently and constantly asked, while jumping up and down, "When will the ice cream be frozen?"

That year, the last year that we had ice in the icehouse, was the year that I recall Uncle Andy, Aunt Grace and their children, Edna, Harry and Eva joined us for the Fourth of July festivities.

* * *

Between the icehouse and the house, was the chicken house, a 100-foot long building. The original wooden-sided shingled shed-roofed chicken house was 50 feet long. The shorter north side wall were probably six feet tall while the wall on the south side was ten feet tall. The tall south side of the building had large windows for light and warmth from the winter sun when the chickens remained inside. This, the original portion, had lath and plastered inside walls, and a dirt floor. A tall wire fence encircled the chicken house to contain the chickens when it was not safe for them to wander everywhere in the barnyard.

Later another 50-foot addition was added. It was the same design as the original, except the walls were not finished inside with lath and plaster. The method of constructing a lath and plaster on the inside wall was to nail laths (1 inch wide strips of wood nailed about a half inch apart horizontally or diagonally) on the inside of the 2x4 inch walls. The lath covered with plaster—a lime mixture was used in houses to finish (or seal) the inside of the walls. The theory was to provide a warmer building with an air pocket between the lath and plaster and the outside wall. However, enclosed walls provided a pocket, a perfect haven for the mice.

Those varmints were such a nuisance as they dug holes everywhere in the floor and walls. How they gobbled up the chicken feed! Mama tried to get rid them with cyanide gas (a very poisonous white powder spooned into the varmint's dens), traps set under baskets, and flattened tin cans nailed over the holes. She even plastered the holes closed. All attempts to shut out these varmints were a waste of time.

The chicken feed was cracked corn and other grains and crushed oyster shell supplement (the crushed oyster shells were the size of corn kernels or smaller). The hens needed the calcium from the oyster shells to make firm eggshells. (Mama washed and dried empty eggshells. She nibbled on them because she said she craved them. I do not know if calcium supplements for humans were available then or not.)

The summer when I was ten, Mama asked me to help her plaster the holes in the walls. She showed me how to use a trowel to apply the fresh wet plaster to the dry plastered wall. With beginner's luck, the new soft plaster would not stick to the dry wall. I laid down the trowel, filled my hand with plaster, and began to spread it on the wall. Unknown to me, I slid my hand down the wall over an flattened old rusty tin can that had been nailed to the wall. I had not seen the sharp rusty tin point that protruded from the wall. That tin point cut my right index finger from the tip to the first joint and nearly to the bone. The tin can had been nailed over a mouse hole years before.

I cried when I saw blood gushing from my throbbing finger. We rushed into the house with blood dripping from my hurting finger. Mama poured clear cold water over my hand, and then tightly wrapped my finger with a clean white rag filled with flour. I passed out as I lay down on my brothers' old bed. I do not know how long I was "asleep." Mama returned to the chicken house to use rest of the wet plaster before it set.

Mama kept a flock of 100 white Leghorn laying hens to provide spending money during the months when there was no income from the livestock or corn. Farmers depended on the income from the cream, and eggs during the winter months. In the fall, the corn, hogs, and cattle were sold. This income paid the mortgages, purchase more livestock, or new farm equipment.

* * *

When I was eight or nine years old, the outhouse was moved from west of the house and attached to the east side of the chicken house. However, we were to use the outhouse only when we had company. Mama said that it was too much work to clean out. Toilet paper was an old Sears catalogue. Instead of using the outhouse, a person looked for a private hiding spot. That spot could be in the chicken house, behind the chicken house, in a barn, or behind a barn. Then corncobs served as "toilet paper."

We, also, had the convenience of inside facilities for nighttime nature calls. A large white enamel cup-shaped vessel trimmed in bright red was kept under Mama's and my bed. The top edge flared flat for a comfortable surface. A large flat curved handle on the side made moving it easy. In addition, we had a blue-gray enameled "slop" jar (styled with bail handle) with a matching lid that was used during illnesses. Sometimes it was used during the daytime in the coldest stormy weather. The one discouraging feature—either vessel had emptied outside the next day regardless of the weather.

* * *

A big old tall cottonwood tree (the Nebraska state tree) stood west of the chicken house. I think it was at least 35 feet tall. Every year, after the tree bloomed, wee bits of "cotton" attached to the seeds fluttered through the air. These tiny cotton-fluff parachutes carried seeds and formed little pools in every low place. One kind of caterpillar loved that tree. I picked them from the tree and played with them. Cottonwood trees grew along the streams and creeks all over the state but rarely grew out on the open prairie.

* * *

The tour of the farm animals' homes ends as we enter into the yard through the north gate. The Chinese elm trees that were planted in the yard when I was around five years old grew quickly to 20-30 feet tall. Sadly, blight came and killed most of the trees about 10 years later.

* * *

Our underground cement-roofed food storage cellar was about 20 feet north of the house. A stovepipe vent extended above the roof to allow for ventilation yet a cool musty odor greeted all who entered. Here was storage space for the home-canned food, plus the winter supply of apples, potatoes, carrots, cabbage, and turnips. The carrots and turnips were usually stored in lightly dampened sand to prevent the vegetables from drying out. Eggs were stored in the cellar. In the winter, it was rare for the temperature to drop below freezing except when the outside temperature remained below zero for several days. A lighted lantern provided enough heat to prevent freezing.

One day I dashed down into the cellar to get a jar of tomatoes. I quickly pulled back the curtain that shaded the shelf of canned food. As I reached for the jar, I saw a blur out of the corner of my left eye. Instantly very sharp toes zipped up my left hand and arm. What a shock! How frightening! I grabbed that jar and flew up the steps to tell Mama about that mouse. Who was most frightened? The mouse? Or was it me?

* * *

Mama kept the incubator in the cellar and hatched baby chicks for several years. A kerosene-powered incubator stove provided the heat to keep the eggs at the correct hatching temperature. Everyday we pulled out the trays of eggs, and turned them just like a setting hen would turn her eggs. After 21 days, it was always delightful to see an eggshell move slightly, and then begin to crack. Soon a little yellow beak would appear quickly followed by a whole baby chick. I loved to hold the new chick very carefully after had it dried into a little ball of yellow fluff. White Leghorn chickens have yellow babies with yellow legs and beaks.

Before the eggs were placed into the incubator for hatching, Mama "candled" the eggs. To "candle" an egg, it was held against an oval opening in a metal chimney (this metal chimney was shaped similar to a glass chimney on a kerosene lamp) that set on a lighted kerosene lamp base. The purpose was to check if the egg was good. If the egg was clear, it was a good egg. If it was dark, the egg was considered rotten and discarded.

When Mama wanted to hatch her own eggs, it was necessary to have roosters in the flock for fertile eggs. We had to watch the hens very closely to make sure they did not sneak off and lay eggs in a nest of their choice. I searched daily in the granary, the hog house, horse and cow barns for eggs. Even then, the hens sometimes "outsmarted" us with a nest hidden in an unseen place. We learned about the unseen nest when the hen appeared with her brood of fluffy baby chicks.

When a "clutch of eggs" (10-20 eggs) was in the nest, the hen would incubate her own little flock of chicks. A mother hen was a cautious mother. If she found food or worms as she scratched in the dirt, she would call her babies with a "cluck, cluck" sound; they would run to her to share in the feast. If a hawk circled overhead, she would squat down, spread out her wings, and call her babies with a different sound telling them to hide under her. Those babies obeyed immediately. Sometimes a chick just could not wait and would stick its head out through its mama's feathers to check on the surroundings. An amusing sight!

When I was older, Mama purchased the chicks from a hatchery in Lincoln, Nebraska. The mail carrier delivered the boxes of day-old chicks to the house. One or two hundred day-old baby chicks provided a chorus of "peeps" for the carrier.

Then our work immediately began, we carried the babies in the shipping boxes to the brooder house west of the house. The clean warm brooder house, heated with the hooded kerosene-burning brooder stove, kept the floor warm. (A brooder stove was a stove designed with a large shield around it to direct the heat down on the floor.) Clean sand was on the floor. Millet (a tiny round yellow grain) was scattered on the floor and placed in shallow pans for the hungry babies. Jar lids or shallow pans held water. The hungry chicks pecked away immediately offering a chorus of "peeps" for every peck. I loved to watch the chicks and hold the balls of fluff—but oh, so gently!

The brooder house was near our mulberry trees, which grew west of the house. The largest tree was the red or black mulberry. I liked the black mulberries, but they were not as sweet as the white mulberries. The white mulberries were the sweetest when a light kiss of purple blushed the plump white berries. These berries did not grow on a tall tree, but on a rather shorter tree more like a tall shrub. I could hardly wait until the berries were ripe. However, there was one drawback with all the mulberries. The berry structure, many tiny cells packed tightly together, allowed dust and grit to become embedded into the fruit during the dusty windy days. That grit could not be washed out. They were often gritty. They were so flavorful and luscious that I ate them anyway.

Not far from these mulberry trees was a row of black currant bushes that grew in a long horizontal row from the mulberry trees out to our lane. I do not recall that we ever picked more than a few currants any year. However, the bushes were useful as they "caught" the snow and formed a drift away from our lane. That helped to keep our lane passable during the winter blizzards. It was the custom to plant rows of trees along roads and highways to catch the drifting snow. This helped keep the drifts from the roads.

* * *

After Mama forfeited her garden for my brothers' hogs, we had a small garden within the fence around the grapevine at the base of the windmill, and in the flower garden south of the house. Some of the different plants in the garden south of the house included castor beans, a beautiful foliage plant, hollyhocks with big colorful flowers, and even two peach trees grown from seed. Fruit trees rarely survived here because of the severe winters. However, these two peach trees not only survived, but also produced a crop of nice luscious peaches for several years.

I was around nine or ten when I begged to plant a garden. My dad plowed the garden space with a plow pulled by two horses. He draped the reins tied together, around his neck and walked with both hands on the plow handles. (I always wondered how he tolerated the reins encircling his neck, as he walked behind the plow.)

This garden was located west of the house in the area that Mama had buried money in a green glass Mason jar the previous summer. One day she said, "I have a hunch I'd better move that money." She did.

A few days later, after she returned home from the Thursday auction sale, she noticed that the area where the glass jar was buried had been disturbed. The loosened soil showed that someone had looked for her cache of over $700.00. Mama suspected my brothers, as they frequently came home asking for money for their trucking operation.

After the collapse of the financial system that closed all the banks in 1929, Mama did not trust her money in a bank. Then she hid any extra money in different places and usually kept some pinned in her under-garments.

Now, back to the garden. To supply water for the garden, an extra stock tank was set on a platform at the base of the windmill. I collected extra pipes that were lying around the barnyard, connected them together, and laid them on top of the ground out to the garden to provide water. I enjoyed tilling the soil with a hoe, planting the seeds, watering, and watching the wee plants grow. My garden was a mixture of vegetables, flowers, and always too many weeds.

We did not grow spinach or any other type greens except leaf lettuce, but an ample supply of lamb's quarters (a weed) grew in the fields and along the fence rows. Mama and I harvested milk buckets of these weeds and prepared them for cooking. Bacon was a breakfast meat, so we always had bacon drippings. Mama placed bacon drippings in a cast iron skillet, filled the skillet with freshly washed lamb's quarters, and in a few minutes, a tasty "vegetable" was ready to serve. It had a wonderful taste, was inexpensive, and better than spinach. However, we could only use these lamb's quarters in the earliest weeks in the spring before the plants became bitter tasting.

Many butterflies visited the flowering plants around the house and in the gardens. I decided to catch and mount them for a butterfly collection entry at the county fair. I used alcohol to kill the butterflies. My collection contained 10 -15 specimens. Fair time was near.

Early one evening, I saw something in my garden that I thought was a large butterfly tasting my flowers. I quickly dropped the metal potato-ricer sieve over the insect. Wow! How my finger began to burn and smart! I yelled and dropped my "sieve butterfly net." My finger began to swell in seconds. I never learned what I had disturbed, but it certainly was not a butterfly! The next day a check of my collection of butterflies revealed that little moths had invaded my collection and ruined every butterfly. All that remained was a few odd wings, and insect skeletons. No fair exhibit!

CHAPTER III

NON-FARMING ACTIVITIES ON THE FARM

Blizzards were very common in December, January, and February. The icy cold northwest wind swirled mounds of the icy snowflakes into drifts upon drifts. Winter winds roared fierce and frosty from the northwest. It nipped the nose, froze the toes, and chilled the bones even through the heaviest coats. The wind drove the snow into our home around the windows and left miniature snow drifts on the windowsills. Jack Frost decorated the windows with gorgeous delicate frosty artwork that vanished like magic when warm temperatures prevailed. The ground was frozen solid.

A typical year on our farm started in January, although very little actual farming was done at this time of the year. The work involved preparation for the farming activities that actually began with corn planting in May. These tasks included—butchering a hog, harness repairs, fence building or repairs, seed corn selection, and other tasks too numerous to recall.

* * *

The cold winter days in January and February were harness repair time. Broken parts were repaired, or replaced and all of the harness oiled. The bridles and collars needed the most attention. My dad brought pieces of the harness into the kitchen to repair, because he did not have a warm shop in which to work. I dreaded having the harness in the house, because the unpleasant odors of horse sweat obliterated the pleasant odor of tanned leather. It was not unusual to see a leather horse collar tucked in a corner waiting for repairs.

41

Butchering

One of the cold weather activities was the annual butchering of a fat hog. Without refrigeration, farmers used nature's cold, frosty weather to protect the fresh meat. Butchering day was a big event. The modern convenience of electricity had not reached western Nebraska in the 1930's and 1940's where I grew up.

The night before butchering day, my dad honed the butcher knives on a small stone until the knives had razor sharp edges. The 200-300 pound hog selected was isolated from the rest of the herd. It had no food or water. Butchering day morning the hog was hit in the head with a sledge hammer or shot in the head with the 22 rifle. Immediately after the hog fell, the throat was slit open to let the blood drain while the final preparations were made. The butchering began after the morning chores were completed and breakfast eaten.

The car was moved from the car shed (common name for "garage"). This shed provided the building for the butchering. The sandy dirt floor required no clean up. A 50-gallon steel barrel was set up on cement blocks near the car-shed door and filled with water. A fire kindled under the barrel quickly heated the water near to boiling.

A chain hoist (metal lifting device), mounted at the top of the derrick (a triangular framework made of 2x4 inch wood that was 20 feet long) hung over the barrel. The hoist provided an easy way to raise or lower the carcass into the near boiling water.

A rope block and tackle (a wooden lifting device) was attached to the cross beam in the doorway of the car shed. Under it were two sawhorses with wide boards laid on top to make a table. (Sawhorses were portable legs made with 2x4x24 inch wooden legs bolted together in an X and attached to a longer 2x4 top bar.) The butcher knives lay on this long table. The washtubs and a large dishpan plus milk pails of fresh water were set nearby in the shed.

As soon as the water in the barrel was near boiling, a can of lye (a caustic disinfectant) was added. A wooden bar, forced between the hog's hind legs, held the legs apart. This bar tightly tied to the tendons of each leg near the hoof provided a bar to grasp and drag the carcass to the large hook of the chain hoist. Now the carcass was hoisted, and slowly dipped, head first into the scalding solution. An unpleasant odor arose when the hog and hot lye water made contact. The scraping of the skin to remove the hair was tested. During the dipping process, the person had to be careful to avoid splashing the scalding lye water on his skin. It could cause severe burns. This process cleansed the animal of mud and dirt and softened the hair. It took two men to handle the carcass during this process.

After the scalding, the men carried the carcass to the table within the shed where they quickly began scraping off the hair and any remaining dirt. Clean water was always available to rinse the carcass and the knives as needed. I carried several buckets of water that were used to rinse the carcass. After the scraping process was completed, the whole carcass hooked onto the wooden block and tackle in the shed, was hoisted up until it was about two feet above the ground. A cut was made on the underside from the slit in the throat down across the belly and onto the tail. This cut was made carefully as one would not want to accidentally cut into the intestines causing unnecessary cleaning of intestinal contents from the carcass.

The intestines were removed first and dropped into a washtub. The other organs - the heart, liver, spleen, sweetbreads, and kidneys were removed and placed in the dish pan, or a bucket and then taken immediately to the house.

Now, the carcass lay on the table after a shower of clean water to remove remaining scrapings. It was time to dismember the carcass into hams, shoulders, sides, backbone, and the head. The feet were removed and saved. I took the parts to the house for safekeeping—away from the dog and chickens. The skin remained on all the parts. The head was dropped into the large dish pan or a wash tub. All the cuts were taken into the house. The next day the cooled meat, the shoulders and hams, were trimmed. The trimmings were reserved for sausage.

Now the meat was ready for the dry curing barrel. This big clean wooden barrel reserved for meat curing each winter was kept north of the house for the full value of the cold January weather. A layer of coarse smoked salt covered the bottom of the barrel, then a layer of meat, the largest pieces—hams and the shoulders were placed at the bottom of the barrel. A thick layer of salt was pressed onto the sides of each ham and shoulder, as it was stacked in the barrel. More salt was packed around and between each piece until the meat was completely buried in salt. The tenderloins, backbone and ribs were saved for eating fresh. The sides, or bacon-to-be pieces were added to the curing barrel. The cheeks or jowls from the head were included. When the jowls were cured, they tasted like bacon. The tight fitting lid covered the barrel. The lid was held in place with a heavy rock.

The curing process took several weeks. The cured smoked hams and shoulders kept until warm weather; sometimes we had the cured ham in July. This dry curing process removed the moisture from the meat. Some people used only salt, and then hung the hams, shoulders and sides in a "smoke house." In the smoke house, a slow burning fire of hickory wood would be kept burning for days to give the meat the tasty hickory smoke flavor. It was a safe place to store the meat and other food products from the varmints and other animals. We had no smoke house, so we used the smoke salt in the wooden barrel.

The meat scraps (trimmings from the hams and shoulders) were ground with a hand powered food grinder. Salt, pepper, and sage were added to the ground meat before it was formed into patties. These patties, small cakes of the ground meat, were fried in the iron skillets, until well done. They were ready to serve. Now they were placed in clean dry one-gallon tin Karo syrup pails, and covered with hot fresh-rendered lard. The lard rendered while the sausages fried. The next day, after the contents of the pails had cooled, the tight fitting lids were put in place. The over night cooling allowed the heat to escape and not form condensation within the pail. The pails were stored in a cool dry place. The sausage was ready to serve after it was heated. When we ate the last of the sausages in late spring, often the meat had a stale taste.

Some people ate "tripe," the cleaned hog stomach. The intestines when cleaned for eating were called "chittlings." We did not use either the stomach or intestines. Sometimes the intestine was used for sausage casings, but we did not. One year, we did try to hand stuff the ground meat into cleaned intestine by hand. (That was probably my wise idea.) It was a very tedious job, and wasted a lot of time. A sausage press, similar to a hand food grinder, but with a special attachment forced the ground meat into the casings. We did not have a sausage press. Mama said that it was easier and quicker to make the ground meat into patties, which we did.

The fat trimmings, the cooled fat meat, was cut into very small pieces, and fried (cooked) in a skillet until it was golden brown. As the meat cooked, the fat (lard) oozed out and left crisp brown "cracklings." Rendering lard was a very hot, dangerous process. A skillet of hot fat could easily catch on fire, or if the hot fat splashed on a person's skin, the results could be a deep burn. We used lard for cooking, while the cracklings were used for snacks, baking, and for soap making. All the moisture had to be removed, or the lard would not keep. Mama poured the hot lard into dry gallon tin syrup pails. The smell or taste of stale rancid lard was very repulsive. Rancid (strong) lard had only one use—soap making. It was never wasted. Rendering lard always left a hot greasy odor that lingered in the house for days.

The head was not wasted. The ears were removed and singed (hair left from the scraping was burned off), then scraped, scrubbed again with a scrub brush, before they were tossed into the cook pot. The teeth, still in the jawbone, received a through scrubbing with a scrub brush and soap, and rinsed, and then the jawbone was added to the cook pot with other meat scraps. The contents of the pot were cooked until the meat fell from the bones. After the bones were removed, salt and pepper were added and then the cooked meat cooled. The fat was skimmed off the top. The meat now called "head cheese" was sliced and served cold. It was yummy. I especially liked to chew the crunchy delicious gristly ear.

The skull bone was sawed in half to extract the brains. Some people liked brains scrambled with eggs. I preferred brains cooked in salted water with a little vinegar. Add a little milk for a dish that tasted like oyster soup.

The tongue, scrubbed thoroughly with soap and the scrub brush and rinsed, was simmered in salted water for two hours. The thick rough skin peeled off leaving delicious lean meat that was thinly sliced and served cold. The only part of the head not used was the eyes, and the squeal.

The feet, singed to remove the remaining hair, were scraped and then scrubbed again. The hoofs removed and the remaining parts of the feet were cooked. Then they were packed into sterilized jars, covered with a hot brine of salt and vinegar, and the jars were sealed. Pickled pig's feet were delicious!

The tail, after it was singed (the hair burned off) and scrubbed again, was cooked with vegetables for a delicious soup.

Butchering was not just one-day's activity; it often involved many days of work. The meat was shared when neighbors helped each other with butchering, then no one had an over supply of fresh meat. I do not recall butchering at our house involving any of the neighbors' help. However, we did share some of the liver and backbone with the neighbors. That was a common practice.

When I was six or seven years old, I began helping with the easier tasks. I brought buckets of the smaller pieces of meat from the car shed to the house and rushed back to get the fresh meat out of temptation of the hungry dog. I carried buckets of fresh water from the well. However, the men did the actual scraping, but I was involved with the meat processing in the kitchen and I watched the whole process.

I always felt sorry for the hungry look of our farm dog whose tail wagged constantly, while licking his chops in anticipation—just a taste, or maybe a feast. Even the chickens kept returning for their tidbits; I chased them away. However, these sideliners received a reward at the end of the day as they shared the intestines, stomach, and lungs. The reality was that not one part of the hog was wasted. Farm families recovering from the Depression wasted nothing.

Cattle

The earliest activity of the year related to the cattle was the calving. During the late winter months, when the calves were expected, the cows were checked daily. If a cow appeared near calving, she was kept in the corral or the barn to prevent her from wandering far out in the pasture to birth her baby away from the herd. The alone-in-the-pasture dangers to the newborn calf were freeze to death or being eaten by the coyotes. If the cow had a birthing problem help would not be immediately available. Every lost calf meant a loss of income.

Before the cattle were driven to summer pastures, all the calves were dehorned. I recall that the horns were sawed off with a dehorning saw. I never watched this process but heard the calves bawling. In 1931 or 1932, a new product came on the market. It was a salve, which was rubbed on the horn "nubs" (The spot where the horns grew as the calf grew older.) when the calf was only a few days old. The salve removed the "horn nubs." This was less painful for the baby calf and less labor for the farmer. Both processes required that the calves be checked daily for two to three weeks to make sure the sores healed. In addition, all the bull calves were operated on, and their testicles removed. These altered calves, now called "steers," fattened quicker for market in the fall.

I do not recall just when my dad began branding our cattle. I believe it was during the early 1930's after news reports highlighted frequent cattle "rustling" (stealing) during the summer pasture season. At night, men would come with a truck and a cattle chute, load up several head of cattle, and disappear. Some ranchers lost several hundred head of cattle during the summer. To counteract this "rustling," farmers began using state registered brands to mark their cattle.

The branding process took two or three men and a hot fire to heat the branding iron red-hot. The fire was built on the ground. The red-hot iron was pressed on the upper hip of the cow or calf disabled on the ground with ropes and held until the branding iron was applied. Smoke curled as the hot iron singled the hair and burned the skin. The cattle carried the scar brand for life. These registered brands proved ownership for each farmer. I dreaded branding day and hated to hear the cattle bawl (cry) from the burns.

As soon as the grass in the pastures had grown tall enough for grazing, selected cows and calves were driven to the pastures. The northwest pasture was a one fourth of a mile from the house. The larger pasture was on the old Cline place, which was about a mile from the house. Each pasture had a windmill to provide water and a block of salt, but no shelter was available to protect the animals from the sun or rain. Care was needed not to put too many cattle in each pasture because then the grass would be grazed down into the ground. Then sagebrush (a woody desert plant) claimed more areas and the soap weed (yucca) plants multiplied. The livestock did not relish these weeds.

It was my job to check on the water in the northwest pasture. Our mailbox was next to the pasture fence, also, the gate to this pasture. When I picked up the mail, it was my job to walk down the hill to the windmill and check on the amount of water in the stock tank and size of the block of salt. My dad took care of this chore at the larger pasture on the old Cline place. The livestock needed a constant supply of fresh water.

The well in this northwest pasture was in a valley at the foot of a hill. I had reported that the supply of water was very low. At noon that day, my dad took the Model T car to the pasture. He parked the car on the slight incline of the hill with the rear wheels nearer the well. He left the engine idle, and then jacked up the left rear wheel in preparation to use the spinning rear wheel as power to activate the pump jack. Then the rod in the well was connected to the pump jack. The belt was placed over the car wheel, then on the pump jack pulley and the engine speeded up. Soon water was pouring from the pump spout into the water tank. He walked home and told me to wait about an hour and then go the well and turn the motor off. He went back to the field work.

I followed his request, as I walked to the pasture, a thought occurred to me—"Wouldn't it be nice to surprise him when he came home from the field this evening to see the car in the driveway?" I left the motor running and carefully disconnected everything. I knew that the left pedal was the clutch, the right one the brake and the middle one reverse. I tried to be careful and not to press down too hard on

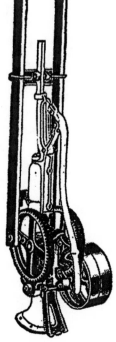

This device that was connected to a hand pump and to the spinning wheel of the Model T to pump water for the cattle in the summer pastures. (Illustration courtesy of Art Haldeman)

the gas pedal, which was to the right of the brake pedal. I wanted to keep the car under control.

That car started rolling backwards! Fear seized me! I knew there was only one thing to do—I hit the brake pedal and turned the key to off. I quickly departed for home and never voiced a word to Mama. Dad walked after the car after supper and he never said anything either. He could not help but know that his ten-year-old daughter had failed. I was so disappointed

In the fall, we rounded up the cattle, herded them back to the barnyard and the home pasture. Immediately the larger steers were sold. My dad loaded up six or seven steers in the truck and drove to the Thursday Livestock Auction in Benkelman, where they were sold to the highest bidder. If my dad saw an animal that he wanted, it was brought home in the truck. The smaller steers were fed corn to fatten them before they were taken to market.

A chute was required to load the cattle into a truck. The cows, one or two cows at a time, were forced to walk up a portable "chute" on wheels into the truck. The chute was a wooden floor with strips of wood nailed crosswise on the floor to provide traction and with sides to contain the animals as they walked up the chute into the truck. I do not recall how long the chute was, but the floor was slanted from the ground up to the truck bed floor. It was difficult to entice the animals to walk up the incline, but we pushed, shoved, and prodded each animal until it was in the truck and the opening in the livestock rack truck bed closed.

Feed bunks were located inside the cattle corral and outside in the nearby pasture area. I believe these feed bunks were about three feet tall and three feet wide and possibly ten or twelve feet long. Two by four inch lumber and two-inch by six-inch lumber was used to build these feed bunks, which had to be firmly braced. The cattle always greedily pushed against the bunks to get to their share of the feed. The feed was ground corn with supplement, or silage. A bountiful supply of hay, salt, and water were always available. The hay, during the winter months, was loaded on a hay wagon from the stacks and hauled to the pasture area just outside the corrals, and pitched onto the ground. The horses and cattle munched until it was gone. This process was repeated every day during the winter months.

Both the cow barn and the horse barn were cleaned every morning. The cleanings (manure) was stacked outside the barn in a pile. When the weather warmed and thawed the manure piles, it was time to scatter the manure on the fields. It was loaded into a wagon and scattered in the fields with a scoop shovel or a manure fork.

Later my dad purchased a used manure spreader. The manure spreader was a wagon equipped with moving discs and shredders at the back that shredded the manure as the horses pulled the spreader. Inside the bed were chains along each side with right angle-shaped metal strips between the chains attached in a ladder-like design. The chains moved from front to back inside the bed, down under the wagon bed floor, and back up to the front of the wagon floor. When the driver arrived at the field, he would pull a lever that set the mechanism in motion as the horses pulled the spreader. The load would "fly" out the back onto the ground. What a quick, simplified method to process a dreaded unpleasant odorous task to one less dreaded. This manure was the only fertilizer my dad ever used. The chicken house was cleaned in the spring, also.

Fences

During the earliest pioneer days, cattle roamed free on the open range. As more settlers moved west this became a serious problem, especially for farmers. Fences became necessary to keep the range cattle separated from the farmers' cattle and to protect gardens and crops.

The barbed wire fence was the most frequently used and was the most economical fence. The wire, named for the short sharpened pieces (barbs) of wire looped over one wire of the two or three strands of smooth wire as it was twisted together. The sharp "barbs" scratched and punched into the necks of animals when they were trying to crawl through or under the taut wires.

Pasture fences required repairs the year around. They were constructed with the barbed wire and fence posts. The posts might be small trees, three to four inches across (small cedar trees or black locust trees were favorites), or larger trees split into usable pieces about the same size as the small tree trunks. The posts were seven to eight feet tall. Holes were dug in the ground about the same size as the post and two feet deep with a post hole digger or spade. After the post was set in place, the hole was filled with the fresh soft earth then the soil was tamped (pounded) down firmly. The posts were set about a rod (16 ½ feet) apart. The space between the posts was measured by stepping sixteen and a half long steps to the next post. The "long step" was estimated to be about a yard long was a convenient measurement.

Gates were necessary to allow entrance into the pasture. Cattle were driven in or out of the pasture through the gate. Teams of horses and even drivers of cars used these gates.

Each gate was constructed with three or four strands of barbed wire that were attached securely to one of the gateposts (a larger stationary braced post) at one side of the opening. Metal staples, sharp "U" shaped nails, were placed with one leg of the staple over each side of the wire and then hammered into the post. The other end of the gate wires (length of the wires was the width of the opening in the fence) was wrapped around and then the wire was twisted tightly on the separate smaller post. To close the gate, the bottom of this small post was inserted into a loop of a heavy smooth #9 wire that was securely attached near to the bottom of the opposite braced stationary gatepost. Next, the top of this small post was pulled against the top of the opposite stationary gate post and secured with a loop of smooth wire slipped over the top of the small post. Presto!—a removable part of barbed wire fence that could be opened and closed like a door.

When I was four years old, my dad asked me to accompany him as he drove the Model T to the northwest pasture. He stopped in front of the gate that was located at the start of an incline leading to the valley to the where the well was located. The wagon wheels had worn ruts in the road. Rains had washed the sand away making a greater incline. He stopped the car near the gate, and left the motor running. He quickly jumped out, and rushed towards the gate. When he was about even with the hood of the car, he realized the car was rolling down the incline. (He had not set the brake.) He jumped in front of the car and spread his arms out as he dug his heels into the soft sand. The car pushed him backward against the gate.

As the sharp barbs pierced his back, he screamed at me, "Put your foot on the brake, and turn off the ***** engine…" I was frightened to see him in that position. I had no idea what he wanted me to do. Finally, I did something, probably turned the key to shut off the motor. I do not recall how he got out of that "pickle." However, he did.

After he checked on the water supply for the cattle, we returned home. When Mama saw his torn shirt and pierced back, she screamed, "You stupid fool! Elsieferne could have been killed! Why didn't you shut off the motor?"

As my dad walked out of the house he replied, "I didn't want to crank that***** car again and risk getting my arm broken." (These cars often backfired during the cranking process. This meant the whirling crank could hit a person and break an arm or leg.)

* * *

After automobiles became popular, another type of gate was required. Often the county road, a wagon trail, snaked through the pasture. To prevent cattle from leaving the pasture through a gate left open, "cattle guards" or "cattle guard gates" were installed.

A "cattle guard gate" was constructed using a shallow excavated square pit, about eighteen inches deep. Cement poured into a frame made with wood around the top of the pit was the base for the gate. The cement frame was six to eight inches wide. Before the wet cement had hardened, iron pipes the length of the desired gate were placed about every four inches lengthwise in line with the fence. Cattle and horses were afraid to walk across the pipes. The "cattle guard gates" relieved an automobile driver the need to stop the car, get out, walk to the gate and open it, walk back to the car, drive the car through, stop, walk back to close the gate and then walk back to the car.

The gate on the left is a regular barbed wire gate, while the one to the right is a cattle guard gate. It was always open for vehicles but livestock never crossed it. (Sketches by the Author)

The summer that I was nine, my dad asked me to help him replace a post that had rotted off in the east pasture fence. The loose post let the taut wires droop. He hitched a team of horses to the wagon loaded with the new posts, staples, and other tools then we headed to the pasture. The rotted post was removed, the posthole was dug, the new post inserted, and the dirt was firmly tamped around the new post.

The wires were stretched with the wire stretcher. (The wire stretcher was a metal tool attached to the next fence post and to the drooping wire. Then a lever was pulled to tighten the drooping wire.) I tried to help staple the wires to the posts. As I lifted the taut top wire to the proper place, about chest high, and tried to fasten it with a staple, it slipped from my hand falling straight down. The barbs caught my skirt, tore it to the hem, and ripped long gashes in my thigh. Blood gushed. I did not have enough strength in my arms to do what I had attempted.

And was my dad angry! He took me home after he stapled the wires to the posts. If the wires had been left unstapled, the cattle could easily have gotten out. Rounding up cattle was difficult. Mama was angry when she saw me. This ended my barbed wire fence repairing.

CHAPTER IV

FARMING

Corn was our main crop, the first crop planted, and our cash crop. The planting began around May 10, the earliest freeze-free date for this area listed in the Farmer's Almanac. My dad followed the Farmer's Almanac planting guide religiously.

My parents' farm contained only eleven hundred acres, which included both cropland and pasture. It was one of the smaller farms in the area. Most of the other farms were three or four times larger.

My dad selected the seed corn in January. Some farmers purchased their seed corn, but my dad chose ears from the bin of ear corn. He selected long heavy ears with straight rows and deep seeds with no smut (a disease that turned the corn kernels to black dust). He brought one five-gallon bucket of these ears into the house each night.

After supper, he would carefully inspect the ears, then with his sharp pocket knife pick out any kernels that had been eaten on by those ugly corn ear worms, or that were not perfectly shaped. He would bite into the kernels. Why? I have no idea.

Next, he would shell each ear by hand by rubbing the corn kernels off the cobs. I think he had some kind of metal hook on his hand, because the top of the corn kernels were sharp and rough. This process continued night after night until he had several bushels of seed corn for planting.

In the mid 1930's he purchased a small iron one-ear-at-a-time hand-operated corn sheller that simplified the shelling process. The sheller had a large rough wheel with a handle that was attached to the side of a sturdy wooden box. As the ear of corn was pushed into the ear-sized iron cone, it

A photo of a hand corn sheller like my dad used to shell his seed corn.

was pressed against the rough wheel, which tore the kernels from the cobs. The kernels fell into the box and the cob fell into the same box. I enjoyed helping shell the seed corn with the sheller.

Planting

In Dundy County, corn was the most widely grown crop. The strong winter gales whipped winter wheat to "death." Spring wheat did not survive.

A lister, a combination plow and corn planter, was the best corn planter for the sandy soil. The two plow moldboards anchored together formed a "V" with the smooth surface inside the curved side was placed at an angle to throw the soil up and made a deep furrow. A hollow shaft, secured between the two moldboards, was attached to a gallon-sized metal canister at the top of this shaft. This allowed the corn kernels to be planted as the plowing was done. A flat disc with holes in it large enough for a kernel of corn to rest lay in the bottom of the canister With these discs, a farmer regulated the number of kernels of corn that were planted per foot in each row. As the lister moved across the field the disc, holding corn kernels, turned to release just one kernel at a time.

Two small upright discs anchored behind the hollow shaft turned the loose soil and covered the corn kernels with the fresh damp earth. Two sets of the plow-planters anchored in a frame made up the lister. Two rows were planted each time the lister was pulled across the field by a team of six horses. The seat for the driver was above and between the two planters. A lever to lower the plowing-planting mechanism was near the driver.

* * *

Russian thistles and tumbleweeds were a nuisance weed because they grew into big round many-branched structures. During the winter, these

54

weeds collected at one side of the field especially if a fence provided a barrier along the side of the field. These weeds had to be burned before the field was planted.

One clear morning in early May (School was out.) my dad said, "You come to the east field and burn the thistles today so I can plant the corn?" Wearing my big brimmed straw hat, with the kitchen matches in my pocket, and carrying my pitchfork, I rode in the wagon with him. He drove across the cow pasture to the east field and then he tied the team of six horses to the pasture fence before he helped me pull some of the big weeds away from the barbed wire pasture fence at the south side of the field. Then he returned to the horses, hitched them to the lister, and began to plant at the north side of the field.

With my pitchfork, I pulled more of the weeds into a nice big pile; there was no wind. I threw a lighted match into the weeds. Instantly a very hot fire blazed. In a few minutes, the weeds were a small pile of light grey ashes. The sun was hot. My job was finished.

I started to walk the two miles home. When I was nearly home, I quit sweating. My head felt swimmery and my eyes were blurry. I was a very frightened ten year old. I thought, "I must get home." Finally, I sauntered into the house, which felt so nice and cool. A drink of water moistened my mouth, but I was very tired, so I went into the bedroom to rest. As I started to lower my body on my brothers' former bed, everything went black before my eyes. I do not know I long I was asleep, or passed out. I felt fine when I awakened. Mama never knew of my strange experience.

* * *

Mama told this story about her brother, Uncle Andy:

"As Uncle Andy, a young man, bravely walked home on a narrow wagon trail on a dark cold windy December night, he thought he had heard something coming towards him. Uncle was brave, but the hair of the back of his neck stood erect while chills raced up and down his spine. His nerves were on edge. "What could that be? Was it some huge beast coming?" He imagined. Faster and faster, it came; it was getting closer and closer!

"Finally, he pulled his little pocket knife from his pocket and opened the largest blade ready to defend himself from the attack of the approaching "beast." As he held the knife in his right hand ready— a huge Russian thistle rolled past."

* * *

When I was in high school, farmers were encouraged to try an alternative crop—milo, a sorghum cane. It grew well during our hot dry summers and had the feed value equal to corn. My dad tried the milo. It was a short sturdy plant with large seed heads. It was planted with the lister. The milo seed, smaller round seed, needed a seed disc with many smaller holes in the seed canister than was used for the corn. I do not recall the harvesting method that was used, or the success of the crop. I know it was planted for several years.

Cultivating

The next process for the corn was cultivating. This began as soon as the small plants had grown tall enough to be seen over the deep brown ridges. Four horses pulled the two-row cultivator. The cultivator had small shovels at the end of iron arms located to the back of the driver's seat. The purpose of cultivating the corn was to stir the soil, knock the ridges (top of the furrows) down, and destroy the weeds.

I recall the year I was eight, Mama was cultivating the field on the old Cline place. It was fun to walk bare-footed in the freshly stirred soil as I followed the cultivator from west to east in the field and back again. For some reason, I do not recall why, I looked behind me and saw a coyote following me. That was frightening! I watched that animal very closely, I had no place to go. I could not safely ride on the cultivator, and I did not feel safe in the wagon. After a few minutes, the coyote disappeared. The next time we saw the coyote, she was sitting on the side of the small hill watching us from inside the pasture fence, just beyond the west end of the cornfield. Mama said, "I bet she has a den of pups near by."

It was unknown for a coyote to attack a person, and I do not recall of instances of that happening. However, coyotes loved to feast on just-born baby calves, chickens, turkeys, cats, and occasionally a farm dog.

Our neighbor, Frank Graham's adult son, Frankie was walking in his pasture that spring. They had an English Shepherd farm dog. Frankie heard footsteps behind him and did not think that anything was amiss as he thought his dog was following. However, for some unknown reason, he looked back and saw an open-mouthed coyote very near his heels. I do not recall how he frightened the coyote.

Back to the cultivating. The corn was usually cultivated two times. The first time was in June and the second time in early July. After the second round of cultivating, the corn was referred to as having been "laid by." (Meaning the planting and cultivating were completed; now wait for harvesting.)

* * *

Sorghum cane, foliage crop for cattle feed, was planted with a drill after the corn. I am not certain whether the soil was plowed before the seed was planted. The drill, a horse-drawn planter, was similar to the lister, except instead of planting just two rows at one time, several rows closer together were planted. I do not recall if the cane was fed to the cattle in the same form as it was cut with the mower, or if it was ground and fermented like silage.

Harvesting

During the 1920's and 1930's single men roamed from farm to farm during the corn harvest. Some were homeless; others were working and saving money for their families. These "field hands" usually came along riding horse back. Their possessions were simple: a bedroll, change of clothes, a rifle, their horse, and a saddle. The rifle was for protection from hunger. They hunted wild game and cooked a meal anywhere they traveled.

The hired men were called "huskers" or "pickers." A husker took a wagon with a team of horses and headed to the field very early every morning, while the frost still clung to the shucks. The wagons were equipped with "throw boards" or "bang boards," which extended one side of the wagon above the regular wagon bed. These "bang boards" kept the ears of corn thrown by the husker from missing the wagon.

The horses were controlled by voice command of the husker. The commands were "gitty up" when the team needed to move forward and "whoa" when they were to stop. The horses were contented to walk slowly between two rows of harvested stalks nibbling on any stalks that they could reach. At the end of each row, the husker grabbed the tied together reins that hung over a stick at the front of the wagon, and guided the horses into the next row. The team moved forward a few steps then stopped to nibble the next bite of corn stalk top. However, occasionally a rabbit darted out from a hiding place, or pheasant flew up in front of the horses and frightened the team. Then the frightened horses galloped wildly away. The horses could injure themselves, or wreck the wagon. Fortunately, those incidents were rare.

The huskers pulled the ears from within outside husks that were attached to the corn stalk, and then threw the clean husk-free ear into the wagon against the throw-board. They wore either a "peg" or "hook" on their right hand.

The "peg," a small metal rod, with attached leather finger loops fit on the hand under the mitten. The rod end protruded out through the mitten. The rod of the peg lay on the hand between the finger joints closest to the hand, leaving enough flexibility to allow the hand to close easily.

The "hook," a metal hook, fit flat on the palm of the hand with the metal hook centered near the thumb area of the palm. It was worn over the glove or mitten. The wide leather strap buckled at the back of the hand and wrist held the "hook" securely in place. With either a "hook" or a "peg," a picker could quickly gouge into the husks, grab the ear, and strip the husks off the ear and toss the ear into the wagon. This husking or picking process continued until the wagon was filled. A good husker could harvest at least two big loads a day, sometimes more if the crop was good.

Husking mittens or gloves were made of a heavy cotton fabric covered with a nap making it look and feel like very heavy cotton outing flannel. They were warm and sturdy yet required many patches during the picking season. Husking mittens and gloves were made with two thumbs. When one side wore out, the mitten was turned over to use the extra thumb on the other side. This way a glove or mitten was worn for more than one day of husking.

The skin on the husker's hands took a beating. With work starting at sun up, the frosty shucks and cold dry temperatures, the skin would crack and sometimes bleed. A popular hand lotion called Huskers' Lotion was applied every night before retiring. The husker's back, arms, and wrists were stressed with every ear of corn picked.

The Author wears a "hook" on her hand in the photo to the left. A "peg" fit nicely in her hand in the right photo. Both tools were used to husk corn. (Photos courtesy of Pauline Caldwell)

Noon brought a welcomed break for both the horses and the huskers. Our huskers relished a warm meal at noon, while the horses rested and refreshed themselves with a long drink of water at the water tank. When the husker drove to the barnyard for dinner, the corn was unloaded into the slatted bin or a fence-sided bin. The harvested ear corn continued drying in the dry fall air.

Corn husking season provided a pleasant musical rhythm with the bang, bang, bang of the ears on the throw boards along with the "gitty ups" and "whoas." Those pleasant sounds created a comforting melodic chorus especially noticeable during the early morning hours.

The goal was to have the corn harvest completed by Thanksgivings Day before the winter's snows. When snow fell while the corn was still in the field, the stalks fell over and much corn was lost. Rabbits and pheasants feasted on the corn when the stalks were down on the ground.

We grew a small amount of blue corn or "Indian Corn," for hog feed, because it matured earlier than the regular field or white corn. Mama and I picked a half wagon load in the early fall for the hogs. This was fun for me, as I loved to hear the sounds as I ripped into the husks with the "hook" strapped to my right hand, then threw the ears "bang" into the wagon.

With the ear corn in the bins or in piles on the ground, drying continued. The kernels, when very dry, were easy to remove from the cob. Next task was corn shelling, which usually happened late in the fall or early winter

* * *

Corn shelling machines were expensive. These big machines were moved slowly from farm to farm with a tractor. The tractor provided the power to run the machine for the shelling process. In the early 1930's these tractors had big steel wheels with 3-inch long protrusions called "lugs." These "lugs" on the tractor wheels tore up the roads and were soon outlawed. The manufacturers replaced the metal wheels with huge rubber tires. These tires were a challenge to inflate without an air pump. Service trucks with special equipment came to the farm.

Corn shelling day arrived. Several of the neighbors came to help. One or two men scooped the ear corn into the hopper (large funnel-like opening) on the corn sheller. The ears moved into the machine through specially designed rollers. This process removed the kernels from the cobs and the remaining husks. The shelled corn poured from a large spout into a wagon or a truck. The cobs fell into a pile at the side of the machine, while the husks were blown into a large pile on the other side of the machine. The owner of the sheller kept checking the machine and belts to see that everything was operating properly. He made sure all the moving parts were well oiled and greased before beginning each day. Depending on the harvest, the shelling process could take more than one day at each farm.

The corn crop provided food for the livestock and a cash crop. Money from the corn that was sold paid the mortgage(s), and was used to buy supplies, including coal for winter fuel. The cobs provided fuel for cooking and heating the house, and husks were fresh fillings for mattresses.

The women prepared feasts of meat, potatoes, beans, breads (always homemade), and homemade pies, and cakes with plenty of black coffee. Everyone looked forward to corn shelling as it was a social time for all. I do not recall having help from the neighbor women. Eight or ten men worked to keep the sheller busy.

* * *

During the worst drought years, the corn was sometimes harvested green. If the farmer decided by August that the ears would not provide enough feed for the cattle during the winter, the corn was salvaged by making it into "silage" or "ensilage."

A sled, a platform made with boards on skids and wide enough to cover two corn rows, was built to provide a place for two men to stand and space between them for the cut corn stalks. As the two-horse team pulled the sled through the field, one man stood one on each side of the sled with a big corn knife (a big heavy very sharp knife about 36 inches long including handle). They quickly slashed the stalks and piled them onto the sled. These stalks were taken to the barnyard and chopped in the hammer-mill. A gray Fordson tractor with four metal wheels powered the hammer mill. I do not recall the year my dad purchased this tractor but I believe it was in the late 1930's. (Foolish as this may sound—this tractor—the Fordson had four wheels and the larger back steel wheels were fitted three-inch long lugs. However, while I was in high school, my dad purchased a three-wheeled green Oliver tractor to use in the farming operation. This tractor had big rubber tires on the wheels. I used this tractor to chop corn stalks with a disc one year in the mid 1940's).

My dad used our empty icehouse for the silage and filled it to the roof. However, there was a problem. The icehouse door was small and that made filling and removing the silage difficult. The heat and moisture fermented the chopped corn. In six to eight weeks, the "silage" or "ensilage" was ready to feed to the cattle. They relished the warm food on cold snowy winter days. Steam rolled off the hot silage as it was spread in the "feed bunks."

Some of the farmers dug big trenches in the ground, filled the space with the chopped corn, and then covered the contents with tarps. The chopped corn fermented converting the corn to the delectable feed for the cattle.

One or two years, my dad had our corn cut with a one-row horse-drawn corn binder after the ears were ripe but not husked. This saved the stalk, the corn picking, and corn shelling processes. We did not own a corn binder. Therefore, he hired a man to do the cutting and binding. This machine cut the corn, tied a bundle of stalks together with binder twine, and then dropped the bundle onto the field. We gathered these bundles, stood them on end (cut end of the stalks stood on the ground), and made corn shocks. When feed for the cows was needed, we hauled these bundles to the barnyard and fed the cattle. The cattle would eat the ears and the stalks, while the hogs ate the corn off the ears and chewed at the stalks. The uneaten stalks served as bedding for the animals. Sometimes the bundles were chopped in the hammer-mill for cattle feed.

* * *

The first year I attended school the sand burs were abundant. They may not have been any worse than usual, but I had not been in the habit of walking through patches of them until I walked through the cornfield on my way to and from school. My stockings were always covered with those burs. I stepped where there appeared to be fewer burs. There seemed to be no way to avoid these nasty burs.

I met the corn binder about halfway across the field as I was cutting across the corn rows. The kind man stopped the horses, and asked me if I wanted to ride to the end of the row where I could walk without so many burs. I said, "Yes." It was so much easier to walk in the grassy area at the end of the field.

However, when I arrived home that night I heard all about my ride. Mama told me that the man laughed and laughed about me sitting on his lap as I rode to the end of the row. Oh, how cruel that seemed. I felt so embarrassed because she laughed. Yes, I had disobeyed her. Again, I learned that I had "sinned against God" for my disobedience. That was the first time I ever remember of sitting on a man's lap.

Haying

Early August in southwestern Nebraska was the haying season. Farmers cut the native grasses, the most available inexpensive winter feed, for horses and cattle.

The following equipment was used: a mower—to cut the grass, a rake— to gather up the dry grass, a hay wagon—to haul the hay (dry grasses) to the barn, or to the place where it was stacked in large stacks near the barns, and four-pronged pitchforks. A team of horses and several workers were needed to use the equipment as appropriate.

The mower blades, flat pentagon-shaped cutters, were very sharp. The cutters were sharpened on a foot-powered round grinding stone. I do not recall exactly the size of the large grinding stone. It was mounted on a short axle that was anchored between two pieces of wood that formed the legs similar to the sawhorse legs. A piece of an old tire, nailed under the wheel, made a pocket to hold water. The water coated the wheel as it turned and cooled the metal to prevent it from getting hot and losing the "temper," or hardness. A seat, from an old piece of farm equipment, was attached to the frame behind the grinding wheel. Under the wheel were two wooden pedals, which when pushed downward like bicycle pedals, turned the wheel. The object being sharpened was held at an angle on the edge of the stone. The turning stone shaved off minute layers of the metal and left a sharp edge.

The mower had a gear-driven sickle bar. The pentagon-shaped cutters, sharpened on two sides, were attached to a long flat shaft called - a sickle bar. The sickle bar slid back and forth through the three-sided protective pointed metal shields as it slid from side to side cutting anything that it contacted. The gears were connected to the wheels that drove the sickle bar. The mower's smaller wheels allowed it to be low enough to the ground to leave uncut grass stems two to three inches tall. The sickle bar, when not in use, was lifted upright forming a right angle to the ground. The driver sat to the left side of the cutting bar. He had to keep his eyes just ahead of the sickle bar to make sure that only grass was in front of the cutting blades. A team of two horses pulled the mower.

The newly cut grasses were slick to walk on, but provided a wonderful aroma, pleasant to the olfactory nerves. After several days drying in the scorching August sun with hot southern breezes the grasses, now called "hay," was ready to rake.

The rake, sometimes called a "dump rake," had large semi-circular prongs or teeth slightly flattened at the end that touched the ground. These teeth were attached to the large 10-12 feet long shaft. The operator sat high above the shaft. A large wheel anchored each end of the shaft. A two-horse team walked as they pulled the rake. The loose hay soon filled the curved teeth. When the curved teeth were filled, the driver would trip a lever and "dump" the dry grasses. This left a long cylindrical pile. These "piles" were placed end to end to form "windrows" across the field. When the windrows were lying in even rows across the field, the field had a unique corduroy-like appearance.

Loading a wagon was easier when it could be loaded from both sides as it was pulled from one end of the field to the other between the windrows. After the hay was in windrows, the hay would again be left to dry a few days in the dry air and hot sun.

Before changing the wagon into a hay wagon, the iron-rimmed wooden wheels were removed and a generous supply of black axle grease was applied to the axles. Then the wheels were replaced. Now the wagon was ready to be converted into a hay wagon.

To convert a wagon from a box sitting on the flat floor to flat floor hay wagon required special racks. These racks were made with 2x4s with either horizontal crossbars or an 'X' inside of a frame. The 2x4 pieces of wood, (two inches on one side by four inches on the other side and as long as was needed to reach across the width of the wagon), were secured at the front and back ends of the wagon floor in the special built-in slots in the wagon floor. The hay was piled onto the wagon floor. Two horses were hitched to the wagon, and then the crew of men, each with a good four-pronged pitchfork jumped on for the ride to the hay field.

Out in the field with the hay wagon, the on-the-wagon workers needed to lay the hay just right on the flat wagon bed floor to make a good foundation and keep the slippery grasses stacked on the wagon. No one wanted to lose a load than have to reload it either in the field, or along the road. Usually two workers lifted the hay up onto the wagon.

As the workers on the ground lifted the hay, they were always cautious as they picked up the hay nearest to the ground because small critters liked to hide in the fresh hay. If the critters were rodents like field mice or kangaroo rats, they presented no problem, as they would scamper away quickly when the hay was moved. However, it could be dangerous if the critter were a rattlesnake. These rattlers were ready to "defend" their territory. No one wanted to share a hay wagon with a rattler either. The diamond-back rattlers were poisonous and quite plentiful in the area. Once the wagon was loaded with the hay up to, or slightly above the racks at the front and back of the wagon, the crew climbed aboard. The team was guided to the barnyard. Since we did not have a large barn with a hayloft, the hay was stored outside on the ground in long tall haystacks with rounded tops.

Building a haystack took skill. The hay had to have a correctly laid hay foundation with each added layer kept just inside the lower layer so the sides gradually sloped inward as the stack "grew" taller. This prevented the sides from slipping out. The top layer needed to have a smoothly rounded firm top surface to provide water repellency. These stacks usually were 10-12 feet tall and as long as desired. Some people covered the tops of their stacks with large waterproof canvases called "tarps."

Several farms in the area had large tall red barns with a hayloft for storing hay. Then another method of storing the hay was observed. The load of hay was taken to the barn and stopped under the hayfork that was attached to a windlass inside a short extension of the barn roof. The hayfork in the barn loft was two giant jaws that would grasp a big "bite" of hay, and then close tightly. A horse with a rider on the dirt or cement floor, inside the barn, began pulling on the rope attached to its harness. (If no horse were available to lift the hay up into the barn, several strong men provided the power to lift the hay to the loft.) The men in the loft guided the fork along the track inside the top of the roof to where they wanted the hay. The hay was released and the fork was ready for the next "giant bite" of hay. This process was repeated until the wagon was empty. Soon all of the hay was cleared from the fields. After each load of hay, the loft workers needed to rearrange the hay to make room for all that was to be stored in the barn. The loft was a very hot location in which to work with almost no air circulation. The stored hay had to be very dry. If there were moisture in the hay, the hay could "heat" and cause a barn fire. On the other hand, the moist hay might just lie and mold making it worthless. Our barn was just one story, so I never had the fun of playing in a hayloft.

When I was in my early teens, I built a haystack alone. There was just a slight inward bow on one side; it did not fall down. I had not kept the layers pushed out far enough on that one side. A well-built haystack was a true work of art and engineering. It had straight almost vertical sides and a nice smooth rounded top.

I enjoyed haying. The ride home from the hay field to the barnyard was relaxing. The aroma of fresh smelling dry hay was intoxicating. How relaxing! The swinging and swaying of the load could cause a person to doze off for a quick nap. That was a special treat.

Workers during the haying season were the farmer and his family. Wives in pioneer days worked outside in the fields along side their husbands, as did the children.

* * *

During the 1940's, tractors emerged and became a labor saving tool. Farming with horses soon became a memory.

CHAPTER V

OTHER ACTIVITIES

Our main crop—corn—had been planted, cultivated, husked, shelled, and stored or sold. The hay (prairie grasses) had been cut, raked, and stacked. The cane was harvested and stacked in the barnyard. November and Thanksgivings Day was drawing near; the basic farm work was completed for the year. After the fall round up, the cattle were driven home from the summer pastures. Another on-the-farm activity that the farmers looked forward to during the fall and winter was hunting.

Hunting

Pheasant and quail season began in late fall after completion of the corn harvest. Pheasants were dressed in glistening greenish-brown feathers with a white ring around the neck were so beautiful I hated to see them killed. They were plentiful but difficult to shoot with a rifle. Shotguns left many pellets in the breast. These pellets were impossible to pick out, plus the pellets were wrapped in feathers. I do not recall that any quail were shot.

Jack rabbit season was all year. The ears of these large rabbits were big almost transparent with black trim. They would stand upright on the hind legs to gaze around, if danger were present. They exhibited a big black tail while dashing away. During the dust bowl days, many rabbit-coyote hunts were organized. The drought and the dust storms went hand in hand, because the easy-to-drift sandy soil of this area of the prairie was not suitable for farming. Cultivating the soil destroyed the interwoven roots of the buffalo grasses, which protected the soil. The dust storms rolling clouds of sand and dust were the results of inappropriate farming methods. The sand and dust were deposited everywhere. Due to the lack of rain, grass for the cattle was scarce. The numerous jack rabbits, also grass grazers, were believed to eating the grass that was needed for the cattle.

The coyotes, though numerous and a predator of the rabbits, were not keeping the rabbit population under control. Easier prey for the coyotes was the baby calves, piglets, cats, dogs, and chickens. To fight back, the farmers organized rabbit and coyote hunts throughout the county during the winter for two or three years.

A hunt was organized to cover a specific area of the county. The hunters, men and boys, at least sixteen years old, formed lines along each side of the designated square, and walked toward the center of the square. At least one team and wagon traveled with each line to collect the rabbits and coyotes. Only shot guns or 410 guns were allowed. The plan was to kill the animals as they were seen, or drive them to the center of the square where they were shot. The hunts netted many rabbits, coyotes, and occasionally a fox (rare in this area). These hunts helped reduce the rabbit and coyote populations. The rabbits were given to the county "poor" home to supplement the menu for the residents. I believe there was a bounty on the coyotes, which was collected when the required tail or ears were turned in.

One school day these coyote and rabbit hunters hiked through our schoolyard. Our teacher kept everyone inside just in case a rabbit appeared and a shot was fired. A stray pellet could easily strike an innocent child.

Food Preservation

During the summer, Mama and I were busy canning vegetables in glass jars for winter use. The first vegetable was green beans. The beans were picked, snapped, washed, and packed into quart and half-gallon sized sterilized jars. Green beans were preserved by the "cold packing" method. The canning kettle was set on the stove, the jar rack inserted (this rack prevented the jars from direct contact with the hot bottom of the kettle, which could cause the jars to break), and was filled with jars, and then water was poured in to cover the jars. A hot fire in the stove soon brought the water to a boil. The jars boiled for three hours for quarts and four hours for half-gallon jars. After the cooking time, Mama lifted the jars out of the hot water, set them on towels, tightened the lids, and then let cool. The next day, we carried the cooled jars to the cellar and stored the jars on shelves behind curtains to shield them from the light.

The same routine was followed with tomatoes, except tomatoes an acid food, were only processed for thirty-five minutes for quarts, and about an hour for half gallons. However, Mama cooked the tomatoes on the stove then poured them into the jars boiling hot, then sealed the jars. This was the "open kettle" method. All the fruits were canned by the open kettle method. Mama and I spent most of the summer canning the winter's food supply.

Dill pickles (made with cucumbers) and watermelon pickles were necessary. Jams, jelly, grape juice, and kraut were preserved for winter feasts. Corn was dried and not canned. The hot August sun and hot dry winds made drying corn cut from the cob a quick process that usually took seven to ten days.

During the winter, shelled corn was made into hominy. This was not canned but eaten when it was prepared. To make hominy, the corn kernels were soaked in lye water to soften the hard shells then rubbed to remove the hulls. The kernels were rinsed repeatedly to remove the lye before it was cooked and seasoned. It was a delicious dish.

Soap making

Our laundry soap, lye soap, was made at home using rancid lard or cracklings or a mixture of both, and lye and water. I dreaded to hear Mama say, "Today, we must make more soap for a supply for winter." Indeed, soap making was a project for warm weather when the doors and windows were open.

Into an old iron kettle, Mama put the light brown cracklings (left over fat meat from butchering), lard, water, and the lye. (I do not recall that any of the ingredients were measured.) A hot fire kept these ingredients boiling until it became the consistency and color of thick honey as it dripped from the wooden stirring stick. The hot mixture was poured into corrugated cardboard boxes lined with several layers of old newspapers. After six to eight weeks, the soap had "cured" and was ready to use. The unpleasant odor of the hot lard and lye lingered in the house for days.

Voting

Although voting was not an on-the-farm activity, it was very important to these settlers. I knew my parents exercised this privilege regularly. However, the year I was twelve, they needed to vote early before my school opened and took me with them to the polls. Dad drove past my school enroute to the Austin School, which closed for Election Day. My parents and I walked into the Austin School building and immediately we learned that I was not welcome.

After a brief discussion among the poll workers, they agreed that I would not influence the voting. I was required to sit in a seat at the back of the room. As my parents explained, they could not to leave me home alone and it was too early for me to go to school. There was no place for me except to accompany them. At that time children were not allowed near the polls. After my parents voted, they delivered me to my school as they drove home. I was unimpressed with the voting process.

CHAPTER VI

WILDLIFE

Animals

Coyotes were the largest wild animal I encountered two times as I walked to and from school. The first time was an April morning that I met a coyote licking his "chops" for a fresh turkey breakfast. This coyote had found a turkey family across the cornfield from the Frank Graham home. The turkey gobbler gobbled his loudest, as he sashayed his boldest impressive strut and dragged his wing tips on the ground with his tail feathers spread into the greatest possible colorful fan. The coyote was unimpressed as his stomach growled from hunger. The turkey hen furiously clucked the message of fear to her soft fluffy brown babies, who disappeared like ice on a summer day. I was as frightened as that turkey family. I ran as fast as I could to the schoolhouse about a quarter mile away. Did that coyote have fresh turkey for breakfast? I have no idea, but I did not recall seeing a scattering of feathers when I returned home from school that evening.

The other time I was enroute home when I heard a noise to my left. Next, I saw a coyote speeding after something just as I came to the top of the first of two sandy twin hills. The coyote crossed my path less than ten feet away. I never saw what it was chasing. Frightened, I dashed for home!

Coyotes always howled in the evenings near sun down. It sounded like packs in different places were calling to each other and answering back. Some called it "singing" but it was a time I preferred to be home safe inside the house.

Skunks in their shiny black fur coats adorned with two bright white stripes down their back and tails were dreaded animals. The huge fluffy tails dwarfed their diminutive striped heads. A favorite food was chickens and eggs. They would kill the chicken by sucking the blood from a tiny wound at the neck. Their natural protection was a musk gland at the base of their tail, which when used left a powerful lingering odor. They often collided with the cars at night leaving an odor that lingered for many days.

Jack rabbits or hares were a large rabbit with large ears and large back legs that jumped when they dashed away. They were seen everywhere in the pastures and fields.

Cottontails, a smaller rabbit, always exhibited a large white tail as they dashed away. These rabbits (We called them bunnies.) stayed around the farm buildings for protection from the coyotes. Both the jack rabbits and cottontails were delicious fried.

Frogs usually are not associated with semi-arid areas, but we had frogs. Under the sand in the low places were small patches of clay-like soil that retained water for several days after a heavy spring rain. The collected water remained for two or three weeks. Soon we heard the frogs choruses at night, a spring treat that lasted two or three weeks. The water evaporated quickly and the frogs disappeared. We assumed that the little frogs buried themselves deep in the soil until the next heavy rain, as the ponds did not remain long enough for eggs to hatch and mature into frogs. Without the heavy spring rains, frogs' choruses were not heard. We found tiny toads occasional in our gardens.

Kangaroo rats and field mice found their places in the freshly cut hay, and in the cornfields. The field mice moved into the farm buildings during the cold weather. Regular rats resided in the farm buildings all year feasting on the livestock feed. The slated or wire wall cribs of ear corn were a haven for the rats until the corn was shelled. Then rats fled everywhere.

Snakes were plentiful in Dundy County. The two most common were the non-poisonous bull snakes and the poisonous diamond-back rattlesnakes. I often carried a bull snake by its tail with its head almost touching the ground. However, the rattlers—were dreaded by everyone! Their venom delivered through hollow fangs was lethal and a bite could mean death. Cows and horses were not immune. The cows frequently had swollen jaws from a rattlesnake's bite. The horses had swollen lumps on their legs.

The rattlers were plentiful in the "prairie dog towns." The prairie dog, a small rodent, lived in "towns" in the pastures. They clustered their burrows close together with "hills" of dirt dug out in the formation of the many underground tunnels to form a "prairie dog town." These animals ruined many pastures. They were grass grazers. Horses or cows who wandered into a "prairie dog town" could step into an open burrow and break a leg. Snakes, especially the rattlers, as well as owls feasted on the baby rodents. Fortunately, the prairie dogs did not invade our pastures.

One day on the way home from school, I found a little snake about a foot long. It had coral, white, and black belts around its body. I thought it was so pretty that I forced it into my water jar and took it home to show Mama. Years later, I learned that a coral snake was poisonous.

The only other snake I recall seeing was the little non-poisonous garter snake.

Birds

Birds provided song and color. The year round birds were the English sparrow, meadowlark, crows, and hawks. The English sparrows were such a nuisance. They built their messy nests anywhere a few straws could be tucked. One summer, I robbed a sparrow's nest of three tiny eggs. I broke the eggs. The whites were clear and firm yolks "what a tiny omelet," I thought as I dropped the tiny eggs into a hot skillet. A tiny delicious bite.

Pigeons, another nuisance bird, devoured many insects but they were not welcomed. They are messy, leaving many droppings everywhere.

The western meadowlark, the state bird of Nebraska, was a year round resident. In the spring, I heard the flute-like trill as the male stood boldly on top of a fence post. His puffed out yellow breast was topped with a jet-black "V" necktie that emphasized his white throat. His back was brown. The brown wings were edged with white bars. The black and white stripes on his head were highlighted with a touch of yellow. During my walks to school and out in the grasslands, I never saw a meadowlark's nest even though they were ground nesters. We knew spring had arrived when a meadowlark stood on a fence post proudly displaying a grasshopper in its beak. Grasshoppers were a favorite food.

Summer resident birds included a mocking bird, Baltimore orioles, red-winged blackbirds, blackbirds and brown-headed cowbirds. For many years, a Baltimore oriole pair, adorned in flame-orange and black costumes, arrived in the early spring. Their uniquely constructed basket-shaped nest of horsehair hung in the large Boston ivy wall that enveloped the Chinese elm tree next to the front yard gate behind the gas pump. Their favorite nest building material, long hair from horsetails, hung in abundance on the fences. All summer these brilliant orange and black birds flitted in and out of the attractive green "wall." Their well-built nest, which hung about five feet above the ground, was attached to many vines. I peeked into the vines and saw the eggs in the nest. I never touched the nest until the birds had deserted it in the fall and migrated south.

The mocking bird attracted the most attention. The slate gray and white male bird (a clown) was always "showing off." Early mornings and evenings, he perched on the top of the windmill wheel—the highest peak of the silent wheel. He would sing with all his heart—songs of other birds—and then fly up into the air to attract attention, and perch back on the still wheel and sing the song of another bird. That was so inspiring and entertaining.

The brown-headed black cowbirds followed the cattle wherever they grazed. A favorite food of these birds was insects on the cows' backs. These birds never built a nest or reared their young. It was easier the sneak into another bird's nest, lay an egg and disappear. The unsuspecting birds became "adoptive" parents of the cowbird babies. These "foreign" babies often crowded out the parent's natural babies to become the sole bird in the nest.

Quail, prairie chickens, and pheasants were game birds. We rarely saw the quail or bobwhite, but frequently heard their call of "bob-white" especially in the early spring mornings. The prairie chickens' drumming calls echoed across the prairie just before dawn. This brown bird, about the size of a chicken, remained hidden from view.

(Mama used Arm and Hammer Baking soda. I always looked forward to each new box of soda because inside of each box was a "Useful Bird Card." I collected each color picture of many birds in North America, especially in the United States. I still treasure my collection.)

Flowers

I recall only a few wild flowers that grew besides the desert plants—the cactus, sagebrush, and yucca plants. However, the sweet fragrance wild purple sweet pea (my favorite flower) grew in protected places. Other wild flowers that I recall included the golden rod (state flower), Texas sand bur (a noxious weed) with a small yellow and white flower that hugged the ground (the seed was contained in a hard shell with long firm needles), the beautiful lavender flowers of the Canadian thistles (another weed), sunflowers, and yellow dandelions.

CHAPTER VII

PIONEER MEDICINE (Mama's version)

Pioneers lived miles from settlements and when medical crises befell them, they devised their own potions and treatments. These are all of the remedies that Mama used that I recall.

Liniment: This liniment was the most used treatment in our household. Mama used one cake of camphor gum (a semi clear solid cake which smelled like camphor was purchased at the drug store. Cost ten cents, I think.) dissolved in one cup of turpentine. If turpentine was not available, Mama used coal oil (kerosene). This liniment was our "cure all." It was used to treat puncture wounds (rusty nails protruded from scrap wood scattered about the yard; I frequently stepped on these nails), strained muscles or sprains, sore throats, and deep chest coughs. For the sore throat and coughs, Mama rubbed the chest with the liniment and then covered it with a white cloth bandage.

My first year in high school, just before Christmas, both of my lower wisdom teeth tried to emerge at the same time. My gums so swollen that I could hardly move my tongue and could not eat. Mama went with me to the doctor and dentist; neither treated my problem just referred me to the other. However, Mama came to "my rescue" with her dependable liniment. My throat was rubbed with a generous portion, then a white rag was tied around my throat. Can you imagine attending high school with that camphor-turpentine liniment and the white rag treatment all in place? I did. (No wonder I was shunned by everyone.)

If a rattlesnake bit one of our milk cows, this liniment was the treatment. In a few days, the swelling would be gone. Swelling on the horses' legs received an application, too. That liniment was used to treat every living thing.

Constipation: If I did not have a bowel movement once or twice a day, the treatment was an enema. Sometimes it was just clear warm water, but most of the time Mama used soapy lye soap solution. "You need to git' the germs out of the body." She said.

Worms: Mama said I would grind my teeth at night when I was very young. Mama's diagnosis—stomach worms. Treatment—wormefuge (an over the counter medicine used to eradicate any internal parasite), taken two times a day for weeks. This treatment continued until my teenage years. Ugh! That taste!

Fumigation: After any contagious disease, the house was fumigated. Sometimes fumigation occurred even when there had been no contagious disease. To fumigate—formaldehyde was poured into a jar lid that she placed and left on the hot stove until all liquid evaporated. Everyone left the house. Those fumes burned the eyes, nostrils and throat. One thing for sure, if any invisible life was there, it would have been gone.

Pimples: I had the usual round of pimples that plague all youth. Mama asked her "spiritualist doctor" for a treatment. He recommended one tablespoon of flour, stirred into a glass of water and drink immediately. Ugh! Drink daily until pimples disappear. No way.

Asafetida: Mama purchased this very foul smelling plant root from an herbal catalogue. I was required to wear a small bag of it on a string around my neck. Reason—to keep disease germs away. It may have been effective, as I had no diseases during the grade school years except colds, which I caught from our water supply. I had almost forgotten about that little "bag" until Mrs. Boswell, my eighth grade teacher and I corresponded years later. She remembered me by that odorous "bag." What a way to make an impression on your teacher! She was my favorite teacher!

Garlic: "You got ta eat lots of garlic," insisted Mama. "Raw garlic" was the best. I had to eat garlic just before I left for school because "it was healthful and good for whatever ailed me." She believed that garlic helped control her "self- diagnosed" high blood pressure.

Poultice and plasters: Chest pains or deep coughs were treated with a hot mustard plaster on the chest then the chest covered with a cloth. A poultice could be used on a bruised finger or for an infection. I do not recall the contents of the poultice.

Burns: Burns were covered with a mixture of unsalted butter and sulfur. Apply a generous amount, then apply a bandage to keep the mixture from rubbing off and to keep the heat in. (I learned cool water relieved the burning sensation quickly when I dunked my burning hand into a pan of cool water after I had grasped a hot lamp chimney.)

Bleeding: Severe bleeding from a cut required a poultice. A generous amount of flour or black soot from the stovepipe was placed on a bandage. The injured part was laid on the soot or flour and then the bandage was tightly tied.

Sore throats: A variety of concoctions was used. Hot salt water or hot water with a portion of iodine was the usual gargle. Coal oil (kerosene) was sometimes used as a gargle. Coal oil was poured over a teaspoon of sugar then swallowed quickly.

Dandruff: Rub castor oil into the scalp; avoid shampooing, as that would "ruin" your hair.

Spring Tonic: Every spring the blood needed to be thinned with a concoction of sulfur mixed with black strap molasses. Molasses was tasty topping for fresh bread but mixed equal parts with the yellow powdered sulfur. The taste was changed entirely.

Dizziness: This was a frequent problem for me but Mama had no treatment. Sometimes when I would get up in the morning, my head would hurt and I was so dizzy that I could not see or walk. Soon I would vomit up the bitterest-tasting green liquid. Within ten minutes, my dizziness was gone and I felt fine. Mama called it a "bilious attack."

Boils: I do not recall Mama's remedy for boils but my brothers often had boils on the back of their neck. They had heard of a quick way to "cure" them. When the boil was white on top, they said to take a small medicine bottle, and hold it over a candle until it was quite hot. Then quickly cover the boil with the bottle opening. They claimed it pulled the "core" out every time. They never confessed that they used that method.

Smoking: Neither of my parents smoked. My brothers took up this socially popular habit while they were in high school. Mama never said anything to me about smoking; I recall no words spoken against smoking when my brothers were home. However, one day my older brother, Alvin was visiting. Alvin, Mama and I were in the kitchen. He started to light a cigarette. Mama reached and took the lighted cigarette from him and puffed on it. I was so surprised to see Mama do that. Then she handed it to me, made me put it into my mouth. "Draw in a deep breath," she commanded. As an obedient nine year old, I obeyed as I had been taught. One puff then I began coughing and became sick. Then both Mama and Alvin began laughing and laughing. I became sicker with each of their bouts of laughter. My throat hurt; I was sick to my stomach; I cried. I was angry! I was angry with my Mama—to think my mother, the one person I should be able to trust, would pull such a dirty rotten trick on her only daughter. Then she laughed and laughed when I became sick. When I was older, had I chosen to take up cigarette smoking, Mama would have denied introducing me to cigarettes. It has been very difficult to forgive her.

Nothing was ever said after that incident about smoking or not smoking. When either of my brothers was home, I helped roll their homemade cigarettes. They were cheaper than the manufactured ones. Actually they had purchased a little machine where one would lay a cigarette paper (rice paper I was told) in a curved out place, fill the paper with tobacco from a tin can or cloth pouch, then pull a little lever to compact all into a neat little roll. All that was left to do was to carefully pick up the rolled up tobacco, lick the glue strip on one side, and press it into place. Presto! a very neat smoke in just seconds. What fun!

CHAPTER VIII

FASHIONS

During the late 1920's, fashions began to change from the straight boyish cuts of the "flapper" style to garments that allowed for more comfort. The 1930 fashions were similar to today's classical designs.

While I do not recall details of my garments during the 1920's, a photo of me standing in front of the cherry tree that grew in the garden near the windmill confirms the style of the garments that I wore when I was four. It was a simple long sleeved bloused top over a full skirt with long dark stockings, and well-worn high-topped shoes. I believe these were typical garments for a farm girl.

Four year old Author was looking at the sun as she stood in front a cherry tree in the garden by the windmill. She wore current garments for a farm girl.

The photo below was taken in 1917 shows the garments worn by my older brothers. I do not know if the curled hair was a style for young boys at that time or something Mama chose to do. I wonder—was she yearning for a little girl?

* * *

Lyle (age 2) and Alvin (age 4) dress in the fashion garments for little boys in 1917.

My first year in school, I wore high-topped shoes and long cotton stockings. When I protested the high-topped shoes, Mama said, "You have to wear these shoes because you have weak ankles." My "weak" ankles never bothered me when I walked barefooted all summer. However, I think that was a common belief that children under a certain age had to wear high-topped shoes to support their ankles.

The long cotton stockings always drooped at my knees and ankles because the garters (small elastic bands that fit around each leg) always moved downward with every movement. However, when I was twelve years old, Mama insisted (fashion dictated) that I had to start wearing a corset "to keep your tummy flat." The Sears catalogue showed many corsets with stays with a laced-up back. Mama insisted that I needed one with the stays. Many problems surfaced with that corset as the stays always gouged me. However, that corset had one excellent feature—the short supporters at the bottom of the girdle grasped and held my long cotton stockings in place all day. What a relief! Gone were the baggy cotton stockings! Soon elasticized girdles adorned the Sears catalogue pages. Every woman and girl found those elastic girdles more comfortable to wear.

Stockings changed. During my younger days, it was 100% cotton knit much like our ribbed knit today. The stockings for older ladies was cotton lisle stocking with a seam up the back of the leg in a smoother knit and the leg of the stocking was shaped to fit the maturing leg. That design was to make the leg look "sexier."

Stores on each coast carried "genuine silk stockings," which were a luxury item in the central states. I enjoyed that luxury once when I was an early teen. A pair of silk stockings was a Christmas gift from Aunt Susan (Mama's sister). However, soon after WWII, nylon (a new textile fiber) hose began to replace silk for stockings. Silk was no longer available from Japan, and nylon stockings became an instant "hit." When a store advertised nylon stockings for sale, women and men flocked to these sales hoping for just one pair of that "luxury." Nylon stockings were comfortable to wear and more durable than silk.

White knitted cotton underwear (long johns) covered my arms and legs and kept the cold chills away during the winter. My summer underwear was made of white cotton flour sacks made to look like knee length shorts.

Flour sacks were made from white cotton fabric with dark ink imprinted emblems of the advertising a brand of flour. The ink was colorfast. This fabric was used in numerous ways as recalled by the following poem:

THE FLOUR SACK

Many a little girl of yesterday wore dresses and bloomers
Fashioned of the indispensable flour sack.
In that time long ago, time when things were saved
When roads were graveled and barrels were staved
When worn out clothing was used for rags.
And there was no plastic wrap or bags.
And the well and pump were way out back
Pillsbury's Best and Mother and Gold Medal, too
Stamped their names proudly in purple and blue
The string sewn on the top was pulled and kept
The flour emptied and the spills were swept
The durable, practical flour sack!
The sack could be filled with feathers and down
For a pillow or t'would make a cheap sleeping gown.
It could carry a book and be a schoolbag
Or become a mail sack slung over a nag
It made a very comfortable pack,
That adaptable cotton flour sack.
Bleached and sewn it was dutifully worn
As a bib, diapers or kerchief unadorned.
It was made into shirts, blouses and slips
And Mom braided rugs from a hundred strips.
She made ruffled curtains for house or shack

From that humble but treasured flour sack!
As a strainer for milk or apple juice
To wave men in was a very good use
As a sling for a sprained wrist or a break
To help Mother roll up a jelly cake.
As a window shade or to stuff a crack
We used the sturdy, common flour sack!
As dish towels, embroidered or not
They covered up dough, held pans so hot
Tied up dishes for neighbors in need
And for men out in the field to seed
They dried dishes from a pan, not a rack
That absorbent, hardy old flour sack!
------- Anonymous -------

* * *

During the 1930's the flour sacks changed from plain white with permanent inked brand names to colorful printed sacks with removable printing. These colorful sacks were very versatile. They became durable fashionable school dresses. I begged and begged for a flour or feed sack dress many times. That request was denied; Mama said," You are royalty. You have to wear silks and satin." Her reason was a story that her father, Mike Grams, told:

"Gottlieb Grams, Mike Grams' father (Mama's grandfather) was a high lord in Germany. Gottlieb Grams was a gambler and lost his fortune and his lordship and his home. He took his family and fled to Prussia (Russian Poland) where they lived until his son, Michael was old enough to serve in the Russian army. They returned to Germany." (Further research has revealed that Michael was proud of his five years of service in the Russian Army.)

However, during the years I attended grade school, I recall wearing lovely woolen jackets and skirts designed for women working in offices, and fur-trimmed wool winter coats. Those garments were toasty warm, but were not a style for a school girl. Fashion dictated that women and girls were to wear only skirts or dresses over one or more starched cotton (flour sack) slips.

Wearing trousers or pants of any style was forbidden. Trousers confirmed that a woman had legs. If a lady showed her legs—what a disgrace! I remember begging and begging for a pair of blue and white stripped overalls like my brothers wore. I thought "how neat." Mama finally gave in and bought me a pair. I loved wearing them. (A photo of me wearing my overalls appears in the Introduction as I stood in front of a team of six horses.)

World War II changed fashions for women when they went to work in the factories. Dresses were not appropriate in the factory environment and pants became an acceptable fashion designed garment for women.

Another big change of the fashion trends has been with denim. When I was a little girl, denim was strictly for the working class—a farmer's fabric. (I recall my dad wearing only blue denim bib overalls.) It was fabric just for men's clothing. Today denim can be found in all price ranges of garments from farm workers to the rough and tumble playwear of the young child. It is acceptable as office wear and even in weddings. The uses for denim have exploded into an "any time—any occasion" fabric.

During my high school years, the fashions remained similar to today's classic styles. However, Paris—the fashion setter—dictated hemline length of dresses and skirts. I recall…"hems had to be just below the knee, or 14 or 15 inches from the floor." The neat poodle skirts emerged. They ended just below the mid-calf, a fad style, which I admired but never wore.

CHAPTER IX

RECREATION

"The stars at night were big and bright" and were easily seen on the open Nebraska prairies. After evening milking was finished, if Mama was not too tired, she and I looked at the star-filled heaven. She pointed out the Big Dipper and the North Star, the only constellations she knew.

I recall one summer night when I was seven that Mama called and called me. "Come see the northern lights," she begged. However, I just could not give up the deep sleep I was enjoying. Her calls seemed like a dream, but the next day she reminded me that I had missed the wonderful colorful display of northern lights. It was unusual to see the northern lights and by Mama's description, the light display was outstanding.

* * *

Before I started to school, Mama and I walked the quarter mile to our mailbox and then down the hill to the well in the northwest pasture. We were checking to see how much water was in stock tank. As we walked, she warned me to be careful not to step on the bright magenta-colored cushion cactus as the sharp "needles" could go through my shoe sole. Another of these nuisance plants were the pear-cactus with bright lemon-colored flowers on green pear-shaped leaves and the "soap weed" or yucca plants with tall stalks of creamy-white bell-shaped flowers encircled with a mound of long slender "sword-like" green leaves around the base. Always the greenish-gray sagebrush plants grew everywhere. When I was older, it was my job walk alone to the mailbox, and check on the water. I missed the companionship as I continued this chore. I never understood why—I wondered—was Mama sick?—have I done something to make her angry? Or was she too tired?

* * *

The summer I was seven, headlines in our weekly newspaper, *The Benkelman Post*, highlighted the news—a whale was coming to Benkelman. That was NEWS! None of the people in the area had been to the ocean or had a chance to see a whale. Seeing the whale was a must! My dad, Mama and I joined the throng that arrived in Benkelman to see the whale packed in salt lying on a railroad flat car that sat on the railroad siding track near the depot. The skin on the huge animal was grayish-black. Touching was not allowed. The whale covered the entire length of the flat car. The hot summer sun on the whale produced unpleasant odors. No one wanted to get very close or to stay very long. That odor—I could not describe it, but it was not pleasurable. The fact—we had seen a whale! We had seen a whale in Nebraska!

* * *

Going to town was a change of pace, a few hours away from the farm. Usually when Mama and I accompanied my dad to town, he'd let us off on Main Street in Benkelman and then he disappeared. We would go from store to store in the three-block area of west Main Street where most of the stores were located.

Mama occasionally bought me one dip of vanilla ice cream in a cone. I think it cost a dime. One day, after I had gotten my ice cream cone (it was not finished), we walked into the Rexall drug Store. What a surprise! Sitting at one of the little round ice cream tables was my dad enjoying a dish of ice cream. At that time, drug stores had soda fountains and three or four small round ice cream tables with wire legs and four matching chairs with little round seats and wire legs and back. They served ice cream, sodas, malts, sundaes, etc. (Today this working soda fountain is preserved in the Dundy County History Museum This museum is located in the first hospital in the county that was built in 1940 by Dr. Moorehouse.)

My hand holding my ice cream cone automatically went behind me as we walked through the door into the store. Mama prompted me, "You tell him you like ice cream, too."

I did. Several people in the store observed this interaction. My dad ordered me a dip of ice cream in a dish. (He did not appear happy to do this.) What a special treat to eat vanilla ice cream from the unusual glass ice cream dish with the special little round-bowled ice cream spoon! Oh, my cone? As I sat down my hand automatically disappeared under the table with it. That cone was a bit soggy from the melting ice cream when Mama and I left the store.

While I do not recall all of the stores in the business section of town in 1930's, the ones I recall were all on the west side of Main Street. They were:

The U.S. Post Office, Office of *The Benkelman Post* (our weekly newspaper), Moses Drug Store, and Ireland's Department Store (our main dry goods store). Also, a variety store, a grocery store (I traded a dozen eggs for a pair of cotton stockings at this store when I was six.), the Rexall Drug Store, a bank, a hardware store, and attorneys' offices. Dr. Lewis, the county doctor's office and a restaurant or two. At the south end of West Main Street was the Ough Hotel. It was across the street from the Burlington Train depot. Tall grain elevators were located on each side of south Main Street beside the Burlington Railroad tracks near the train depot.

At one time mail was snatched, during the night, as the train sped through town. The mailbag hung on a hook near the track. As the train zipped through town, a mechanical arm in the train reached out and grabbed the bag as the train whizzed past.

The Zorn Theatre was located on the east side of the street about a block from the stores that I mentioned. (Mama and I attended one movie there *Gone with the Wind,* when I was in high school.) The County Courthouse was on a hill about two blocks from the main shopping area. I believe a Ford automobile dealership and a gas station were also on the east side of Main Street.

Main Street was (and still is) a very wide street. The Census Bureau reported that the population of Benkelman was 1,154 in 1930. (The 2000 census reported 1,006 residents.)

* * *

In the spring of 1938, Mrs. Boswell, my eighth grade teacher, encouraged all of her students to prepare artwork to exhibit at the fair. She kept and carefully stored the pictures at the end of school, then entered them in the fair. When Mama and I attended the County Fair, we viewed the school art exhibits. I was thrilled to see my pictures in the collection from the District #37 School. How delightful to see blue and red ribbons on each of my entries! My entries included: a mountain scene in oil on glass (painted in reverse) with a blue ribbon, a drawing of a big rabbit on which I used colored pencils received a red ribbon, booklet of maps from my history classes, and local bird booklet, both with had red ribbons.

Speaking of painting—Mama loved to paint with oils. Due to the lack of funds and knowledge to buy canvases (not available in Benkelman), she painted on broken pieces of glass. With no art education, she drew or painted excellent landscapes on paper. She taught me how to use lines as shading to produce realistic scenes. I often wondered how she could afford to purchase the oil paints and brushes, as there never was any money for luxuries. Perhaps she had purchased those paints before the fall of the Stock Market in 1929, which was the beginning of the Great Depression.

* * *

August was County Fair time. The fair grounds were across the railroad tracks near the Republican River. Each year we attended one day but left early in the evening to take care of the livestock on the farm. My dad drove to town then disappeared while Mama and I toured the fair grounds. She and I inspected all of the exhibits and noted the sideshows, which we did not attend. Black women sat on chairs in front of their private tents. People of color did not reside in the county.

Of the carnival rides available, the Ferris wheel and the merry-go-round were my favorite rides. Each year I was allowed one ride. However, the year I was 13 or 14, Mama surprised me with, "You can ride every ride." The one ride I had longed to try for several years, "the merry mix-up," was my first choice. Sadly, it became my last ride, because I was so merrily mixed-up and sick from the swing of the spinning seats that turned around and around, swinging out from the center to an almost horizontal plane than around and around again. When the ride stopped, I could not even stand up. I was still spinning after I had both feet planted firmly on the ground. Mama laughed. I was unimpressed.

* * *

In early August, the summer I was seventeen, Mama and I attended the Indian Pow Wow at Trenton, Nebraska. Trenton was a small river town about 30 miles east of Benkelman on Highway 34. The annual Pow Wow assembled in that valley named "Massacre Valley" and recalled the huge loss of life of the Pawnee Indians, who were friends of the white settlers. The celebration reminds everyone of the last battle between the Sioux (a warring tribe) and Pawnee Indians (hunters and planters).

During the Pawnee Indians' fall buffalo hunt in 1883, 700 men, women and children gathered near the location of the town now called "Trenton." The first day of their hunt, they killed many buffalo with their bows and arrows. The women butchered the animals and cut the meat into strips to dry for winter consumption, and treated the hides to use as clothing and tents. However, more meat was needed to provide enough food for the tribe for the winter.

The next day, the Pawnee Indian Braves followed the buffalo herd into the large valley near the Republican River. Suddenly the Sioux (Dakota) Indian Warriors from the north swooped down and massacred the Pawnee, who were out numbered two to one. The United States government had tried to set territory lines for these two tribes. The Pawnee territory was south of the

Platte River and the Sioux territory was on the north side of the Platte, but the Sioux did not abide by the territory lines. The area where this massacre occurred was many miles south of the Platte River.

When Mama and I arrived, we saw many teepees at the celebration with different Indian designs on the sides. The teepees were crude looking. The Indians had decorated their faces with war paint of all colors on their dark oiled skin. They appeared mean and war-like. Their long black hair hung in crude braids decorated with feathers and bones. How strange they looked to us. Their leather clothes, decorated with colorful beads, appeared soiled and grungy. Some of the Indian men were dressed in just a leather lion cloth. They looked undressed. Mama was not impressed with this different culture. I was awed at the sights. However, my memories of that day are vague.

Many booths displayed gifts and mementoes. We purchased nothing, not even food, which was readily available. I do not recall observing any Indian dancing or hearing any drum beating.

* * *

A picnic—wonderful change at this cool restful oasis! Rock Creek, a State Fish Hatchery was located about seven miles northwest of Parks, Nebraska at the site of a natural spring. The fish hatchery and recreation grounds were cool and relaxing. The water trickled and babbled in the rocky creek bed. Birds hidden in the bushes and trees sang happy songs. Butterflies flitted here and there. Different species of tiny baby fish swarmed in many tanks located at this oasis. This fish hatchery seemed out of place in this semi-arid area. My dad, my mama, and I enjoyed a picnic at this quiet restful location just once. I wanted to return but the farm work kept us busy.

CHAPTER X

SCHOOL

The pioneers, though few had extensive education, realized the value of an education. They required schools for their children. One-room school houses, which were built in every township, provided education for all the children in the township. The opportunity for education was close to the homes of the homesteaders' children. The schoolhouse was located, when possible, near the center of the six-mile square township.

At District #37, where I attended school, students from two families were three miles or more from the school. The Ferguson children rode a work horse three and a half miles to the school and were paid a fee for transportation for the days they attended school. Donna's family lived three miles from the school. Her mother transported her to and from school with the family car. Altogether, children from three families' homes rode a horse to school. A barn and hay provided for the horses' comfort. All youth, from the age of six, were required to attend school through age fifteen. The eight-month long school year was designed to allow the older students to help with farm work.

September 1931, Mama said, "You gotta go to school today. You wear that long sleeved brown dress, those new high topped shoes and the long cotton stockings." Puzzled, yet I reluctantly complied. She hurriedly brushed and braided my long hair. After she prepared my lunch, she picked up my shiny new syrup pail lunch bucket and told me to git my penny pencil and pencil tablet. She walked with me through our sand bur filled cornfield south of the house, over the twin sandy hills and onto the grassy area at the end of the neighbor's cornfield until we saw the little white schoolhouse. Mama stopped and said, "You go on. I'm not dressed fit to be seen." She turned and headed for home. I was six and a half years old. I knew my brothers had attended this same school. Yet I had no idea what school was all about and I was afraid.

A frightening day! I knew no one. I had never been around other children. I had never had a playmate, nor had anyone to talk to except my family and that was usually Mama. I had never met the teacher. I was dressed differently than the other children with my plain brown long-sleeved dress, long cotton stockings, and high-topped shoes. My hair was braided. None of the other girls wore long sleeved dresses or long cotton stockings. I was so hot miserable, lonely, and sad.

I was so overcome with fear that I could not talk for six weeks. However, when I started to talk, I was promoted immediately to grade two. The three other little girls in grade one were not happy with my promotion. Our teacher, Mildred Stamn, had thirty-two students, in all eight grades.

Some outstanding highlights of my grade school years were seeing my first magnificently decorated Christmas tree. During third grade observed the eighth grade class solved square root problems on the blackboard instead of solving my long column addition, which I detested. I was pleased when I was allowed to continue writing my letters in cursive, which I had learned before I started to school. However, the most rewarding event was graduating from the eighth grade in seven years.

The lows of grade school included: constantly bulling by the big boys, and learning that Santa, just a man dressed up in a red suit, who never found my house anyway. Teacher's little sister who stole my yellow pencil (a gift from my Grandpa Grams), and broke it before she hit me in the nose, when I asked for it to be returned. Walking to school in the bitter cold weather in deep snow, I was chilled to the bone by the time I walked one and a half miles to school or back home. I was afraid to allow one of my teachers to take me home after she dismissed school early because she feared the falling snow could become a blizzard. Mama had said, "You hav' to walk, understand?" I tried to obey. Watching others have fun playing games, and never allowed to enjoy one of the three swings. School was not a pleasant happy place.

Our school day started at 9:00 A.M. with a recess at 10:30, an hour lunch at noon and afternoon recess at 2:30 P.M. with the day ending at 4:00 P.M. The children played games at recess, but I just stood around watched others play.

When games required sides, I was always the last one chosen. A favorite game was "Andy-Over." The children choose teams. One team had the soft ball, which was tossed over the schoolhouse. We had to make sure the window shades, inside the school, were pulled all the way down as the three long windows on each side of the school were directly across from each other. The windows were the only source of light in the schoolhouse. The shades blocked the teams from seeing the other team's actions. If the team on the opposite side of the schoolhouse caught the ball, that person and team would run around the building and tag as many students as possible of the opposite team. The team who did the tagging claimed the "tagged" students. The game continued until everyone was on one side or the bell rang for the return to classes.

Other outside games included Pom Pom Pull Away, Tag, Follow the Leader, and softball. I never could hold the bat correctly and no one had ever demonstrated the proper way.

The boys played "marbles" and no girl was "smart enough" to know how to "shoot" marbles. The girls jumped rope, played hopscotch, and jacks, but I always longingly watched.

A fun winter game was "fox and geese." After we had at least two inches of fresh snow on the ground, a leader usually the teacher, walked in the clean white snow to form an "apple pie circle" followed by the rest of the students. After the circle was marked, the leader began cutting across the center, then across again dividing the circle into four equal spaces. The center where the paths crossed became the fox's den. The fox was "it" and tried to tag the others to claim them until all the students were tagged.

During the coldest blustery days, recess was inside. Some of the most popular games were: I Spy, Fruit Basket Upset, Tic Tac Toe (a blackboard game), Simon Says, and Blind Man's Bluff.

Holidays celebrated included Christmas with an exchange of gifts between the students. The first year I drew the name of a boy a year older than I. Mama said we had no money to buy a gift so she insisted that I wrap up my only new pair of brown cotton stockings. He was angry to receive "girl's stockings."

Valentine's Day was a fun day. We each made or decorated a container into which all the students placed a Valentine. All of the Valentines I delivered to the other students' boxes, Mama and I made, while most of the Valentines I received were store bought. A package of 25 Valentines cost twenty-five cents and included a special Valentine for the teacher. The teacher had candy treats for each student.

Easter meant—decorated Easter eggs and a fun egg hunt. Every student brought several decorated eggs to school on the day of the hunt. The eggs (hard cooked) that I took to school were hand-decorated and usually dyed with natural materials. I felt so embarrassed not to have bright yellow, blue, green and red eggs like the other students. Mama said we had no money for such foolishness as buying dye for Easter eggs. Keeping the eggs cool was never a consideration as no one had a refrigerator (electricity was not available).

The eggs were hidden outside in the school yard by the teacher and one or two of the older students during the afternoon recess time. The rest of the students stayed in the schoolhouse with all the shades drawn. When someone tried to peek outside, either under or at the side of the shade, the rest of the students inside threatened to "tell." After the hiding was completed, the teacher opened the schoolhouse door and everyone rushed outside, with a sack or a construction paper basket made in art class, to collect as many eggs he or she could find. The teacher always added extra eggs, which were usually candy eggs. Any eggs that were missed that day when found and were eaten after the egg hunt.

I graduated from this one-room school in seven years. Mama apparently had not considered high school even though I begged and begged to go. I felt I deserved the same opportunity that my brothers had as they attended high school as soon as they graduated from the eighth grade. However, students either had to board in the town where the school was located, or drive (a 14 year-old could obtain a driver's license to drive to school), or be driven to and from school daily. Mama was afraid I would associate with the wrong crowd and who knows what could happen. I had to return to the one-room school and take the eighth grade over—what a waste of time! I had my diploma, which the county superintendent made sure I received. She said, "Elsieferne has earned it and deserves to receive it." It arrived in the mail after the county graduation exercises were held.

A year after I had graduated from the one room school, a gentleman, Sam Gourley from Parks, Nebraska, (location of one of the small high schools in the county) purchased a small school bus. He contacted parents of eligible students and organized a 30-mile route (one-way). The high school student enrollment was 60 students that first year I was in high school. Mama finally agreed to let me attend high school, as I would be home every night. I was delighted as this was my dream. However, riding the bus became a daily dread. One night, the boys took my lunch box from the overhead rack, without my knowledge, then laughed, and laughed at the contents (my long cotton stockings that I had removed).

In the spring on the route home, one of the older boys stepped behind my aisle seat, and hit me as hard as he could on the back of my neck with his fist. The blow was so severe that I saw "stars." Mama told me to write to the State School Superintendent about the incident. Then I was in trouble with the Parks High School Superintendent. I told Mr. Kolb, the superintendent that Mama had instructed me to write that letter. Mama finally began to understand that riding on the bus was not safe for me.

During August, before my sophomore year, Mama and I searched in Parks for a place for me to stay. We found an elderly lady, Eunice Knepper, with whom I could board during the week. I was delighted to avoid the school bus although I still rode the bus to school on Monday mornings and home on Friday evenings.

This nice lady evidently had poor eye sight. Her dining room and kitchen were in the basement. Mice occupied the basement and the pantry. Those critters feasted in the open boxes of dry cereal and white rice. The food items were prepared as usual. How difficult it was to eat foods and see the mice droppings in the ready-to-eat breakfast cereals and rice dishes. Ugh!!! I still cringe at the thought.

At the end of my sophomore year, I was determined to graduate the next year. I could tolerate the repulsive environment no longer. Six weeks before the end of my junior year, I became the ninth member of the graduating class.

A very tragic incident occurred three weeks before my high school graduation, my brother, Lyle drowned. He and two friends were fishing at the Imperial, Nebraska, City Reservoir. He challenged them "I'll race you to the other side (of the reservoir)." He jumped in and disappeared from sight. They could not swim but ran to the office some distance away. It was hours before his body was found. It was so sad to attend his funeral just two weeks before my graduation day.

Finally, May 19, 1943, graduation day arrived. I graduated with the full 32 required credits with a grade average of 93 (on a four-point scale). I had achieved my goal—to graduate from high school with full credits in just three years. The moment that I received my diploma, I was elated! I had achieved my goal of graduating from high school. Thus, I had completed my education journey from grade one in the one-room country grade school and through high school. Mr. George Pringle, a member of the school board, gave me the most precious gift anyone received that night when he said, "I think you have done better than all the rest."

What a treasure!

EPILOGUE

After high school graduation, summer school attendance occupied my vacation time between teaching in one-room schools in Dundy and Chase Counties, Nebraska. Before I completed credits for a B.S. degree from Sterling College in 1948, I was married.

In 1993, I attended my 50th High School Alumni celebration. By that time, all the county high schools were consolidated into one high school in Benkelman, Nebraska. The Parks High School Class of 1943 gathered in the Parks Community Building for a bountiful pitch-in dinner and hours of catching up. It was a very rewarding experience. Of the nine graduates, of Parks High School in 1943, all were living except one boy. However, only six attended the celebration. We were asked to write 20 lines of happenings over the last 50 years. The following couplet was my contribution (I cheated with two extra lines.)

MY CHALLENGE

Summarizing 50 years in a nut shell? Wow!
After PHS, McCook Jr., and college was no pow-wow.

The dare of Nebraska's multi-graded elementaries
Was followed by Sterling College's educational adventures.

Here a love bug bit, wedding bells rang,
A Cornhusker became a Hoosier with a twang.

Two new Hoosier gals came to bless
And challenged mom at her best, no less.

Volunteering, church, 4-H, creating toys for the ill,
Substituting, clothing designing, State Fair modeling were the bill,

"Go west!" rang in my ear
My aged mother to be near.

The MA in Special Education from Ball State
Came after she passed through the Pearly Gate.

A goal retired, a home shattered,
Another divorce, another mom now single, not battered.

Grandchildren's care urged from their mother,
The dream departed, I was the do-other.

Therefore Bloomington became my home
Photos examined; wedding gowns altered and sewn.

A way of life in my little nest.
Thanks to many friends, I've tried my best!

By Elsieferne Mendenhall Stout, May 1993

* * *

During a visit to Nebraska in 2003, I planned to show my friends, Lloyd and his son, Michael from California, the home where I was born and resided for 21 years. My cousin, Leroy, his wife, Sue, and my daughter, Ruth, accompanied me. We followed the usual road without seeing the familiar house. Then Leroy suddenly realized that we had just passed the driveway. He stopped and backed up. We saw nothing. The old house had been in need of a lot of TLC was gone. The area was just bare pasture land.

During summer of 2002 my daughter, Ruth, granddaughter, Megan, Wynona, a dear friend, and I had stopped and ventured inside the house. Two or three trees were still growing beautiful and green. Although, all of the other buildings had been gone for years. Now not a trace of anything!

Where were the beautiful elm trees that had survived the elm blight? The trees, a monument of that dedication, which I had faithfully nurtured with gallons of water daily, were now invisible. Not a green leaf was in sight! So sad!

The windmill, the stately beacon to travelers who traveled along the road, was a signal of a haven of refreshment—just a drink of fresh cool water. A blessing to many thirsty travelers. Not a trace of it or the well, but I had known that the well had caved in. The windmill—it had been gone for years.

When had everything disappeared? Why? A puzzle! The home place, my birthplace was still marked a year before. That house and trees stated that someone had lived and survived in this harsh environment. Now nothing survived! Everything was once again grassland.

I had heard that the property, which Mama had sold years before, was now in an estate. In addition, I heard the rumor that the executor of the estate had everything crushed and buried.

Good-bye house! Good-bye, lovely green trees! Good-bye, stately windmill, and well! Farewell! My memories will live on forever! May everything rest in peace!

* * *

The Author's growing up years on this farm in Dundy County, Nebraska, are detailed in *Dundy County Babe* It was published in 2006 by AuthorHouse.

ABOUT THE AUTHOR

Photo courtesy of Pauline Caldwell

I was born in Dundy County, Nebraska, the daughter of Homesteaders. My education began in a one-room school in rural Dundy County, continued at the Parks High School, Parks, Nebraska. I received a B.S. (Home Economics/Biology) from Sterling College, Sterling, Kansas and a Masters (Special Education) from Ball State University, Muncie, Indiana.

One-room schools in Dundy and Chase Counties is where I began my teaching career. Later I substituted in grades K-12 in the consolidated schools in Rush County, Indiana. Currently besides writing, I design my own clothing and am a professional clothing alternationist. I am an active volunteer in my community and church.

While living in Rush County, Indiana, I wrote a weekly community news column for the *Rushville Republican*, the daily newspaper in Rushville, Indiana. The first book, published in 1993 was *My Pioneer Ancestors* (family genealogy included histories of both my parents). In 2006 *Dundy County Babe* (an autobiography of my life on the farm in Nebraska and life in Indiana) was published. *Gitty Up—Whoa* is the companion book of *Dundy County Babe*.

I live in Bloomington, Indiana. I have two daughters and five grandchildren.